NATIVE AMERICAN
SPIRITUALITY

WITHOUT THE TREES, THERE WOULD NOT BE THIS PAPER.
WITHOUT SUN AND EARTH, THERE WOULD BE NO TREES.
WITHOUT GREAT SPIRIT, THERE WOULD BE NO CREATION.
WITHOUT A CREATION, THERE IS NO CREATOR.
WITHOUT A WRITER, THERE IS NOTHING TO READ.
BUT WITHOUT A READER - WHAT NEED OF A WRITER?
EVERYTHING IS CONNECTED.
THIS BOOK IS DEDICATED TO
THE MYSTERIOUS WEB OF LIFE THAT UNITES US ALL.

Thorsons
PRINCIPLES
OF

NATIVE AMERICAN SPIRITUALITY

TIMOTHY FREKE
AND WA'NA'NEE'CHE'
(DENNIS RENAULT)

Thorsons

The publishers would like to thank
Jillie Collings for her suggestion for
the title of this series, *Principles of . . .*

Thorsons
An Imprint of HarperCollins*Publishers*
77–85 Fulham Palace Road
Hammersmith, London W6 8JB
1160 Battery Street
San Francisco, California 94111–1213

Published by Thorsons 1996
7 9 10 8 6

A catalogue record for this book
is available from the British Library

ISBN 0 7225 3333 0

Text illustrations by Tony Meadows

Printed in Great Britain by
Clays Ltd, St Ives plc

CONTENTS

ACKNOWLEDGEMENTS

My love and gratitude to Victoria Moseley for all her considerable help and support in the writing of this book. Also to Peter Gandy for his valued comments and his constant friendship. Thanks also to my agent Susan Mears, and all at Thorsons for their part in helping this little book into existence.

TIMOTHY FREKE

The quotes by Black Elk are reprinted from *Black Elk Speaks*, by John G. Neihardt, by permission of the University of Nebraska Press. Copyright 1932, 1959, 1972, by John G. Neihardt. Copyright © 1961 by the John G. Neihardt Trust.

I would also like to thank Heyday Books for granting permission to reprint material from *Straight With The Medicine* as told to Warren L. d'Azevedo, Heyday Books, Berkeley. Copyright © 1978, 1985.

The quote by Peter Blue Cloud is taken from 'Coyote, Coyote, Please Tell Me' from *Elderberry Flute Song*, Crossing Press, Trumansburg NY. Copyright © 1982.

FOREWORD

Native American Indian Spirituality is based on an understanding that transcends the fundamental organizations of religion. The way we approach spirituality gives us a chance to grow, and to experience life and all that life has to give. We look at this life as a pathway that will lead us back to the whole, to oneness with the Creator. We are here to experience the love of life and to accept the great mystery.

All of us, at one time, have asked these simple questions – Who are we? Where did we come from? Where are we going? – questions which have been asked for centuries by people throughout the world. All mankind and womankind are seeking and searching for the answers. They have asked about mortality and immortality; what direction to take and how to find that direction. Each culture has tried to provide a basic structure upon which to make sense of the meaning of life and somehow justify living. With this in mind, man has created many different religions to try and explain these very questions. However, even with all these religions, people continue to search for answers. Why?

Throughout time, human beings have held on to the belief that there is a greater force in the universe; that there is a greater power than ourselves. This belief system has given people comfort and brought logic and order to their world of confusion and hurt. We feel such hurt and confusion when a loved one has passed on – what this society would perceive to be death – or when an illness takes hold. At these times, we feel that all control has been taken from us. This is the time when we must readjust our way of living, until the body heals itself, before we can continue. It is at these times that most of us are willing to turn to a higher power to gain satisfaction and to regain control over our lives.

However, in the Native American Indian way of life, there is no death, only a passing on. We believe that we are on a pathway to the next world. Whatever happens to us in this world determines whether or not we return to the oneness of the whole: Home. If we do not pass life's tests, then we have to atone for our mistakes. When we come before the Creator, it is not the Creator who judges us, but ourselves. We believe that the Creator is love and that his love will not judge us. We, as humans, have to review our own past and if we make too many mistakes then we know what judgements have to be rendered. We also feel that illness sometimes has to occur to bring balance to our lives, and that this is a time to readjust our thoughts, a time for visions.

Travelling the world has led me to realize that people are still searching. They are searching for truths about themselves. Each individual is trying to find their pathway of balance and understanding, to bring them back to their centre, and to the meaning of life. Each person will ask themselves these questions: how can I make this connection with the power of creation? How can I find the meaning of life? What happens to me after death? This search leads to many pieces of a puzzle. The pieces of this puzzle are to be found throughout the world. People are trying to put this puzzle back together to find the answers.

They have now come to Turtle Island, to find the pieces of the puzzle within the teaching of the people of this continent and within themselves.

The first lesson that we should learn is that religion is a man-made institution, but Spirituality is given to us by the Creator. The people of Turtle Island chose to live in the way of the spiritual teachings and not in man-made laws that were designed to work best for those who control the religious institutions. We did not practise our way of life just on Sundays, we practised it every minute of the day, seven days a week, year in and year out. If we talked it, we walked it.

For years, society has called it a Native American Indian *tradition* or *culture*. They have even convinced many indigenous people that it is a tradition. But I would simply call it a way of life, and it is now time once again to share this way of life with the people of the world. We must come to understand that God comes in many names and forms, but that he is all one and the same, the Creator. Unfortunately, people will say that their way is the only way, that their God is the only God; that only their way will bring you to the gates of heaven. When will people realize that there is but one way, the Creator's way? This way is for all and gives every being the right to choose their path in life. If the right path is picked, then it will lead you to the whole – Home. The spiritual path that we walk does not choose the way for people to believe or to walk their path. One is not condemned for their own beliefs in the Creator. For us, it is very simple; all living things were created by the Creator, therefore all things are part of the whole, and part of the Creator. Many religions try to make it sound as if they are responsible for choosing the chosen people, but in reality it is we, the people, who choose to be chosen.

All life is created by the Creator, therefore all living beings are part of the Creator, part of the whole. We were all created from the earth, our mother. All creation was placed into the womb of Mother Earth. The creator reached out and touched the womb and gave the creation a life force energy – and created *spirit*. *Spirit* became a living part of the earth. At the end of our journey, the body and mind return to the outstretched arms of Mother Earth. If we have walked a good life, then our life force energy returns once more to the source of the power, and rejoins the whole. Never forget that we are all part of the earth, along with all creatures big and small, and that we must learn the value of all life that has been given, and respect, love and care for our Mother Earth.

Among the people of Turtle Island, there is a saying which is common to all Nations of this island: 'To all my relations' or 'We are all related'. This is said after we finish a prayer or a talk, to remind us that the Creator, through love, made fertile all life. All beings that have been, that are in the present, and that will be born in the future; the animals, birds, insects, plants, herbs, trees, rocks, air, water, fire and earth. These are all part of creation, they are our grandfathers, grandmothers, brothers and sisters. We are all one in *spirit* and *energy*, we are all of the earth. We may come in many different forms and shells. We may all have different qualities, gifts and powers. But in the end, we are all one. We are all connected to the circle of life. Once you understand this connection, you will come to understand the source of the power and the Creator. At this time, you will start to communicate with all parts of creation. If we doubt, all we have to do is look around and see that all things are alive, and we can see the Creator in all living things.

As you read this book, understand that it will not answer all your questions. This is only a beginning. This is only the first step on the path to understanding the spiritual connection that each nation or tribe has to creation.

Now, in your thoughts, see yourself walking in a meadow of green grass. As you are walking, you come to a pond of still water. As you stand there, look down at your feet and see a pebble, a small stone. Lean over and pick up the stone. Toss the pebble or stone into the air, towards the centre of the pond. Follow the flight of the pebble, watch as it falls from the air and into the middle of the pond. As it enters, there is a splash, and from the splash a circle is formed. Watch the circle as it makes its way to the shore where you are standing. When it hits the shore, the circle disappears and the cycle of the circle is now completed. But look up and you will see more than one circle coming towards you from the centre where the pebble entered. Think of what you have heard about a circle – that there is no beginning, that there is no end. But with one pebble, one stone, you have found where a circle begins, which is in the centre, and where it ends; at the shore, when its task is completed.

There are many circles in life. We must be prepared to complete one circle and then move onto the next, always getting closer to the centre, to the source of the energy, the meaning of life. With this first circle, you will start the first step in finding your path, the first step in finding yourself. Remember, do not get caught on just one circle; if you do, you will forever be going around in circles. Grasp the knowledge of that circle and then move on to the next. One day you will look up, and you will be at the centre, and the mystery of life will be revealed to you.

WA'NA'NEE'CHE'

INTRODUCTION

Coyote, Coyote, please tell me
what is magic?

Magic is the first taste
of ripe strawberries, and
magic is a child dancing
in a summer's rain.

Elderberry Flute Song – PETER BLUE CLOUD

Native American Spirituality is rooted in a living, vibrant, animate Creation. It is an ancient wisdom, with a proud history, but like the mythical trickster-teacher Coyote, in *Elderberry Flute Song*, it always points to the present; to the magic of an immediate, intimate, personal connection with the natural world.

With this in mind, this book does not attempt to be an historical or academic survey of dead traditions. Rather, it goes in search of the living truths that these contain. There are many voices in this book – scholarly observers and students of Native American ways, like Joseph Epes Brown; voices from the proud Native American past, like Black Elk and Chief

Seattle; and also voices of modern Native American teachers, especially Wa'Na'Nee'Che'.

Native American Spirituality is not dead history. It is very much alive, and teachers like Wa'Na'Nee'Che' are playing a crucial role in helping it grow and change to meet the challenges of the present day. A Sweat Lodge leader and pipe carrier, Wa'Na'Nee'Che' has sat in council with renowned figures like Franks Fools Crow, High Bear, Noble Red Man, Medicine Bear Chief, Black Elk (grandson of the famous visionary, whose presence will be felt throughout this book) and others. However, he is not a 'traditionalist'. He teaches a return to 'The Old Ways' that underlie all Native American Traditions and calls himself a 'Spiritual Advisor' rather than a 'Medicine Man'.

I have sought to spin the threads of these various voices into one yarn. Like, I suspect, many of my readers, I am not a Native American, but someone who has been drawn to the wisdom of the primal peoples of the world, in my search for solutions to the personal and collective dilemmas that confront us in these difficult and confusing times. My role has been to listen carefully to these different voices, and draw out of them an understanding that will bring their wisdom to life; showing the perennial depth and the contemporary importance of their vision.

This book examines the primary principles that underlie the Native American understanding of life. It explores the type of culture within which this wisdom arose. It looks in some detail at particular traditional ceremonies, such as the Sweat Lodge and the Vision Quest. But above all, it attempts to give a taste of the 'magic' that Coyote speaks of in *Elderberry Flute Song*. To this end, I have completed most chapters by suggesting some simple, practical exercises that the reader may like to explore, to stretch their understanding beyond the written word into the world of their own direct experience.

Coming into an intimate relationship with Nature is not always easy for many of us who live in vast, overcrowded cities. But look closely and you will see the grass pushing up through the concrete pavements and tarmac roads. Even here, nature can reach us. While writing this book I visited London; I was choking on the fumes of a hot and busy day, surrounded by impersonal crowds of anxious people, when I saw a poster leaning lazily against a lamppost. On it was an old black and white photo of a solitary and noble Native American, looking wistfully out over never-ending, empty, open plains. Underneath this still and centred figure was written a prophesy of the Cree people. It read:

> Only after the last tree has been cut down,
> only after the last river has been polluted,
> only after the last fish has been caught,
> only then will you find that money cannot be eaten.

Like the grass pushing through the tarmac, the natural wisdom of the primal peoples is trying to reach us through the cracks in our industrial civilization. It is a great irony of our age that so many of the answers to our modern dilemmas of environmental crisis, and loss of spiritual direction, are held by the very peoples who were subjugated as savages, and destroyed in one of the greatest holocausts in history.

This book starts with this dreadful destruction and ends by searching for a life-line for our modern society, from within the remnants of the cultures that it so ruthlessly and carelessly laid waste. This book is about looking back to relearn 'The Old Ways', and looking forward to apply these perennial truths to our present condition.

TIMOTHY FREKE

THE SACRED HOOP IS BROKEN

And so it was over.
I did not know then how much was ended.
When I look back now
from this high hill of my old age,
I can still see the butchered women and children
lying heaped and scattered
all along the crooked gulch
as plain as when I saw them with eyes still young.

And I can see that something else died there
in the bloody mud,
and was buried in the blizzard.
A people's dream died there.
It was a beautiful dream...
The nation's hoop is broken and scattered.
There is no centre any longer,
and the sacred tree is dead.

BLACK ELK – SIOUX MEDICINE MAN

Our present century has seen some terrible crimes. To think of the death camps of the Nazis, for example, is to remember the potential for horror that hides inside the human heart. Now consider, for a moment, the genocide of a whole continent of people. Imagine the wanton destruction of rich and varied cultures that had flourished for centuries. This is not distant history. This was a campaign of terror that reached its final climax a little over a hundred years ago. This is the story behind the formation of the American Nation, the most powerful country in the modern world. And the soul of the modern world will not find the peace it so desperately craves until it re-examines its past, and rediscovers the wisdom of those it reviled.

When Sir Walter Raleigh arrived in Virginia in 1584, he said of the indigenous people, 'a more kind and loving people could not be'. Early Christian explorers speculated that here were human beings so uncorrupted, they must have been untouched by the Fall of Man from the Garden of Eden. The early settlers would not have survived in this new and strange land, had it not been for the help and compassion of the Native Americans who befriended them. After all, this was a huge and abundant land that could be shared.

THE BALANCE IS BROKEN

Into a balanced harmony of man and nature, the early settlers brought disease epidemics, the like of which had never been known by the indigenous peoples. These new illnesses ravaged humans and animals alike, spreading across the continent ahead of the White Invaders, like a premonition of their destructive culture that was to follow. Some estimates suggest that before the Europeans arrived, there were ten million indigenous inhabitants of North America. By the time contact between the races was well established, this number had already been reduced by disease to fewer than one million. It was as if the balance of life had been fatally shaken by the intrusion of this alien culture, which was itself disastrously out of balance with the Natural Ways.

As the White Man's greed for land expanded, he no longer saw the indigenous peoples as welcoming hosts. He reduced them, in his mind, to little more than vermin, to be exterminated by any means. The Native Americans did not understand. In 1609, the Algonquin leader Powhatan asked, 'Why will you take by force what you may obtain by love? Why will you destroy us who supply you with food?' The venerable Potawatomi said to his people in 1831, 'War is wicked and must result in our ruin. Therefore let us submit to our fate, return not evil for evil, as this would offend the Great Spirit.'

In response to the initial forbearance and charity of the indigenous peoples, the 'Christian' Europeans waged war on them. Disease epidemics were even actively encouraged, by the deliberate supply of smallpox-ridden blankets to the native people! General Sherman, one of the leaders of the 'Indian Wars', concluded in 1868, 'The more we kill this year, the less will have to be killed next year. For the more I see of these Indians, the more I am convinced that they will all have to be killed, or maintained as a species of paupers.' By the end of the last century, this is exactly what had been achieved.

Although the European Invaders had superior weapons, their success was not primarily due to military victory. This war was a war of lies and betrayal. Treaties were cynically made, and broken, to suit the short-term self-interest of the White Man. At the end of his life, the Sioux leader Red Cloud recalled, 'They made us many promises, more than I can remember, but they never kept but one; they promised to take our lands, and they took them.'

4

The massacre of buffalo on the Kansas Pacific Railroad
(from a wood engraving by J Berghaus 1871)
(*Peter Newark's Western Americana*)

THE END OF A DREAM

When a census of buffalo was taken at the end of the last century, a mere two hundred were found. Just ten years previously there had been in excess of sixty million! The famous Buffalo Bill alone claimed to have killed 4862 animals in less than eight months. This extermination had initially been wanton and mindless, something the Native Americans were totally unable to comprehend. Eventually it became government policy, with slow trains laden with hunters traversing the Great Plains. This was not done to destroy the buffalo, but rather to remove from the people of the plains their major source of food, clothing and shelter. The indigenous people and the buffalo were both part of the same 'Web of Life' or 'eco-system', and by the relatively easy destruction of the buffalo, the White Man brought the last free Native Americans to their knees.

Total surrender was inevitable. Some tribes, like the Boethuk of Newfoundland, were hunted to extinction. Others were imprisoned on undesirable land, that had been set aside euphemistically as 'reservations'. Native children were beaten in residential schools for speaking their own language. Traditional ceremonies were made illegal. Alcoholism was actively encouraged. As the Sioux Visionary Black Elk put it, when remembering the carnage of the last great massacre of his people at Wounded Knee, a people's dream had died and the 'nation's hoop' was broken.

Dee Brown ends his seminal Indian history, *Bury My Heart at Wounded Knee*, with a poignant image from this atrocity – the bleeding, wounded bodies of four men and forty-seven women and children are unloaded from open wagons in the freezing dark, and dumped on the rough, hay-strewn floor of an Episcopal mission. The year is 1890, it is four days after Christmas, and amongst the decorations above the pulpit hangs a crudely worded banner which reads: 'PEACE ON EARTH, GOOD WILL TO ALL MEN'.

THE STRANGE LIFE OF SITTING BULL

The final destruction of the Native American way of life hap-pened within a generation. There is no story that captures these strange times more dramatically, or with greater irony, than the life of Tatanka Yotanka, the great Hunkpapa Sioux Holy Man and War Leader, known as 'Sitting Bull'. In his early life, Sitting Bull knew nothing of the White Invaders, but he lived to wit-ness them destroy his people. During the Indian Wars he led

Tatanka Yotanka or 'Sitting Bull', from a photograph taken in 1885, while he was with Buffalo Bill's Wild West Circus (*Range/Bettmann/UPI*)

the greatest number of Sioux warriors ever gathered to-gether, in their historic victory over General Custer at the Battle of the Little Big Horn – a conflict he led by sitting in prayer and performing sacred ceremonies. Later, returning to finally surrender to the US Government after exile in Canada, he led a disease-ridden band of only some two hundred people.

This life, steeped in glory and tragedy, was also rich in irony, for the great war chief was, at one time in his life, a star attraction in Buffalo Bill's Wild West Circus! Annie Oakley, another famous circus performer, recalls that he was so distressed by the poverty in the eastern cities of the White Man, he gave away most of the dollars he earned to street urchins and young beggars. In 1890, at the age of 59, he was murdered by some of his own people, now wearing uniforms and working for the US. Government. Some of these had even fought alongside him at the Battle of the Little Big Horn, and suffered with him in exile in Canada. In 1893, Sitting Bull's log cabin was shipped to Chicago, and displayed before 27 million white people, at an exposition to celebrate the 400th anniversary of the arrival of Columbus in the New World.

BARBARIC PAGANS

The 'West was won' by force, by deceit and by disease. But the greatest weapon of the White Invaders, one which allowed them to justify all their actions, was an idea: the idea that these proud and cultured people were savage and uncivilized pagans; that these people were a part of nature and, that, like the 'Wild West' itself, they were to be tamed, subdued, and brought under the yoke of 'progress'. When in 1882, the Pawnee leader Sharitarish said to President Monroe: 'I have grown up, and lived thus long without work. I am in hopes you will suffer me to die without it', the Europeans, their minds bedevilled by the Protestant work ethic, did not see the Red Man as natural and content, but only lazy and backward.

This cultural blindness and cynical misrepresentation has continued into the storybooks and Hollywood films of our own century. The indigenous Americans have been portrayed as cruel scalp-hunters – although this practice was introduced by whites so that bounty hunters could claim money for the 'Indians' they had butchered. They were seen as primitives – although at a time when Europeans still lived as serfs and vassals, the Iroquois had a democratic Six Nation Confederacy, which later inspired elements of the Constitution of the United States. They were patronized as naive nature-worshippers – although their spirituality was deeply profound and centred always around the one 'Great Spirit'.

To European eyes, the native people seemed unsophisticated. But they were wise in ways that their invaders were too foolish to recognize. They were seen as superstitious when they told the settlers that it was important to maintain balance in nature by giving back to the soil when you have taken from it. Now, fifty per cent of the American top-soil has been lost and the land is barren. The native people were ridiculed when they called the trees their 'relations' and said without them all life would end. But now we watch as the world warms and the deserts expand, a situation caused, in large part, by the massacre of the trees.

THE NOBLE SAVAGE

In extreme contrast to the idea of the 'barbaric pagan' was the romantic notion of the Native American as a 'noble savage', living in a primitive, communistic Utopia, perfectly in harmony with the natural world around him. Or he was depicted as the devoted 'Tonto', riding at the side of the Lone Ranger, like a redskin version of the Negro 'Man Friday' by the side of Robinson Crusoe – a sort of butler on horse-back with a

feather in his hair. These 'Indians' are not real either. They are
also the invention of the White Man's imagination.

WHO WERE THE AMERICAN INDIANS?

In fact, the 'American Indians' were neither 'Americans' nor 'Indians'. It was the European invaders who gave the name 'America' to the place the indigenous people called 'Turtle Island', and who gave the blanket term 'Indians' to the many nations and cultures that flourished there. Many of the names by which we know the different tribes are actually distorted versions of nicknames – often insulting or humorous – given by one people to its neighbours. Most tribes called themselves simply 'The People' or 'The Two-Leggeds', or 'The People Who Live In This Place.'

In truth, they were many different nations with many different cultures. There were the nomadic hunters of the plains tribes, like the Sioux, the Pawnee, the Crow; agricultural communities like the Iroquois of the eastern woodlands and the Great Lakes; the fishermen of the Pacific coast, like the Kwakiutl; the urban communities of the peaceful Hopi in the south.

The US Government acknowledges 267 different tribes, but there were in fact a thousand or more tribal groupings, speaking hundreds of languages, some of which are as different from each other as English is from Japanese. Some of these cultures had been established for centuries. Others were the result of more recent adaptations to changing circumstances. The Blackfoot, for example, are renowned as great horsemen, although they didn't come into contact with the horse until 1730.

All these nations aspired to be noble, brave and wise, and they all shared a common spiritual relationship with the Earth

The homelands of some of the Native American peoples

and all Nature around them. But many tribes were also cruel, violent, ethno-centric and male chauvinistic. Some of them owned slaves and horribly tortured their enemies. In short, they were prey to the same faults and foibles as any other race; they were human beings – like you and me. As the old warrior Black Hawk said, when he met President Andrew Jackson, 'I am a man and you are another.'

Both these images – the barbaric primitive, the noble savage – stop us connecting directly with the people of Turtle Island, as an important element in our common heritage of human history. The indigenous people's way of life may have been destroyed, but their wisdom is still alive and relevant today, and to understand this Native wisdom we must first find a feeling for the culture from whence it emerged. We must journey back in our collective memory to an America of vast open plains covered in buffalo; to virgin woodlands teeming with wildlife; to a time when the imagination was not in the service of making commercials for consumer durables, but was animated by visions given by Great Spirit; to a time before the sacred hoop was broken.

LIFE ON THE GREAT PLAINS

A POW-WOW

In the summer months, the people of the great Sioux Nation, one of the peoples of the plains, gathered for what has become known as a 'pow-wow'. These were colourful social gatherings, where many different tribes came together, forming a vast mobile tipi 'town'. Some of the crowd would dress in their ceremonial outfits, with feathers and splendid decorations. The People gathered to celebrate, to share dances and songs, race horses and play gambling games, trade stories and barter goods. As marriage was often not allowed between members of the same clan, these events also gave young men and women of different tribes the chance to meet and fall in love.

Goods were not only bought and sold, but also exchanged as gifts in a ritual 'give-away' or *potlatch*. Here, a person was held in high esteem, not for the wealth that he kept to himself, but for the extent of his generosity. These gifts were not unwanted cast-offs, but useful and well-loved items. This giving was an act of sacrifice, in the original sense of the word, 'to make sacred'. To give in any other way was not deemed honourable. In the winter gatherings of certain tribes, pine trees were decorated with tobacco ties – pouches of sacred tobacco – and underneath the trees the gifts were placed for the winter give-away. Some say this was a precursor of the 'Christmas Tree'.

MEN AND WOMEN

Some of the women would wear the hide of a bison cow, painted in a stylized abstract fashion with an image of female generative power, symbolizing all the sacred medicine of womanhood. Some of the men would wear the hide of a bison bull, perhaps decorated with a solar sunburst motif, representing the sacred powers of manhood. A man may also have carried the left wing of an eagle in his right hand, while a woman would carry the right wing in her left hand. This was a reminder that men and women need each other, for a bird with only one wing cannot fly.

Each sex had its particular *medicine* or spiritual power. Traditionally, a man was often thought to see more clearly in the physical world, and a woman to see more clearly in the 'hidden', spiritual world. It was the woman's role to bring together the *energies* required for sacred ceremonies, like the 'Sun Dance', which the men would perform. Women were often not required to take part in certain purification ceremonies, like the Sweat Lodge (*see Chapter 5*), because their menstrual cycle was seen to purify them naturally, rooting them in Mother Earth and helping to keep them spiritually balanced.

Men and women had certain traditional roles in this society, but these were not rigidly fixed. An individual's particular gifts from *Spirit* were more important. A woman could become a chief, or even sit on a war council. Here, her opinions were valued because it was thought that, as a mother, her experience of love would mean she would seek to avoid unnecessary conflict.

In this spirit, with individuals valued for what they were, homosexuals and transsexuals were treated as 'special' people, and not forced to conform through fear of being socially ostracized. Indeed, they sometimes had their own ceremonies. For example, amongst the Sioux, Crow and Kiowa tribes, the honour of climbing the Sun Dance Tree and placing a sacred 'Medicine Bundle' (*see Chapter 4*) on top of it, as part of the preparations for the Sun Dance Ceremony, was often given to a *Ma-Ho* – a person with 'two souls in one body'. These were either men who displayed female characteristics, or women who displayed male characteristics. It was believed this sacred duty was best performed by a 'special' person who could represent both sexes.

CHILDREN AND ELDERS

Native American culture engendered a great respect for age. In some ways, children were brought up more by their grandparents than their parents, who were busy being providers. And this was seen to be in balance, for while children have just come from *spirit* and are not yet fully of this world, so elders are beginning their return to *spirit* and are also not fully of this world. The elders, having lived long and full lives, had many lessons in survival to teach the youngsters. And they were guardians of wisdom and knowledge built up over thousands of years, passed down through the line of ancestors and added to by each new generation.

The people of Turtle Island did not have our modern problem of inexperienced, heavily-stressed parents rearing children in isolation, away from a supportive community. If a child had no grandparents, other relatives or tribal teachers would instruct them. The old were not seen as redundant or 'retired'. The old and the young were known to have a special relationship with *spirit*. Children with 'imaginary' play-friends were not told to 'grow up', but seen as potentially having the 'gift of vision'.

WARRIORS

Native Americans had a proud warrior culture with a high code of honour. Warriors were charged with the sacred duty of protecting the women and children under their care. Until their wars with the White Man, the greatest warrior was not he who had killed a man, but he who *counted coup*. This could be done in many ways, for example by touching an enemy with a special *coup stick*. By doing this, a warrior showed not just skill and courage, in getting so close that he could have taken his opponent's life, but also compassion and forbearance in sparing it. A Warrior could also count coup by stealing prizes from an adversary – such as medicine bundles, horses, eagle feathers, bows and tomahawks. This 'theft' also displayed his stealth, guile and daring. Before the coming of the White Man, it was not honourable to count coup by taking a scalp, although a warrior may have cut a 'scalp lock' – a piece of braided hair symbolizing the defeated man's *medicine* power – from an enemy.

A warrior displayed his victories in the feathers that he wore (*see chapter 4*), or by symbolic decorations on his coup stick. For example, if he had taken an enemy's horse, he might decorate his stick with strands of the horse's hair. The way he painted his horse and his face also symbolized his triumphs; this gave rise to the phrase 'losing face'. If a warrior claimed courage by decorating himself in a certain way, and then failed to live up to his claims, or showed pride, or exaggerated his achievements, he would 'lose face'. The way he appeared – the way he painted his face – was not the way he was. This was great dishonour.

In some instances, disputes were not settled by war at all, but by sporting competitions. These were often very dangerous, requiring both physical prowess and freedom from fear. Native American culture did not avoid danger, or hide death behind closed doors in hospitals, morgues and abattoirs. These were men who accepted that life is fragile and often short. They saw this 'Earth Walk' as a transitory journey, the purpose of which was to return with honour to Great Spirit. Each time they went into battle they would say, 'this is a good day to die.'

Despite their overwhelming numbers and superior technology, the white soldiers were defeated over and over again by Native American courage, skill and cunning. There is an Indigenous American joke that asks: 'Why does the White Man have a long neck and the Red Man have a short neck?' Answer: The White Man has a long neck because he is always straining to see what is hiding behind the next rock – and the Red Man has a short neck, because he is crouched behind that rock, lying in wait for the White Man!

SITTING IN COUNCIL

The organizing bodies of the tribes were Councils made up of trusted and respected people who had proven their ability to think and act in the interests of all. The council members sat in a circle because, like the spokes of a wheel, every person was of equal importance. Before the business of the Council commenced there would be many prayers and the ceremonial sharing of the sacred peace pipe (*see chapter 4*).

During free and open discussions, every 'sacred point of view' would be heard, and every possibility explored. Any relevant dreams or visions that had been experienced by the participants were considered very seriously. Personal burdens were left outside the Council and any irrelevant disagreements were put aside by 'burying the hatchet'. Sitting in council was a collective process of finding conclusions to which all could assent. Benjamin Franklin and Thomas Jefferson visited the Iroquois Peace Confederacy and sat with the Council of the Clan Mothers of the Six Nations. They were so impressed by the arrangement that they used it as an inspiration for the Bill of Rights.

The purpose of the Council was to bring balance and harmony to The People. If justice was to be administered, it was not important to ascertain the exact details and proofs of a case, as it is in our adversarial law courts. Rather, the view was taken that a certain act had put the whole tribe out of balance, and that this balance had to be restored. No one could 'judge' or 'correct' someone without first 'walking in their moccasins' – without knowing what it was like to be them. A 'guilty' person might be asked to suggest what they could do to restore balance. A man who took another's life, for example, might pledge to support that person's family, or make a gift of horses. If someone would not make amends, they could be exiled from the tribe, which would be like cutting a tree off from its roots.

When someone spoke in this Council, the others listened respectfully, not looking him in the eyes as the Europeans do, but rather bowing their heads, gazing downwards in attentive reflection. While a speaker held the *Talking Stick*, he would not be interrupted. He might pause to gather his thoughts, or listen to the voices of the *spirits* – but no-one would fill the silence or attempt to take the floor. The person who wished to speak next would hold the *Answering Feather*. When one speaker had finished, he would pass the next the Talking Stick, and the Answering Feather would then be available for the next would-be speaker to take up. The proceedings always ended as they began – with prayers of gratitude.

HEYOKAS

Amongst all this respect and solemn ritual was the ceremonial clown, or 'contrary', called *heyoka* by the Plains Peoples and *koshari* by the Hopi and Pueblo. *Heyokas* were respected for their great *medicine*, or power. They were entertainers who also stopped people taking themselves too seriously, and the culture from becoming too rigid. Like Coyote who appears in many myths and stories, they were both tricksters and teachers. Their function was to turn the world upside down. They imitated people to show them their foolishness, seeming to deal in deceit and illusions, while actually mirroring human nature. Through laughter and irreverence they imparted wisdom and self-knowledge.

The job of a 'contrary' was to show another side to life; perhaps performing quite normal everyday activity, but back-to-front – walking backwards, dressing backwards, even talking backwards; riding their horse facing in the wrong direction; using 'no' for assent and 'yes' for denial. *Heyokas* poked fun at respected tribal figures and mocked serious tribal customs, but, like a Shakespearean court jester, they were tolerated and even encouraged. However, unlike the harmless modern circus clown, they could be quite disturbing: frightening and attacking people, waving giant phalluses and performing mock intercourse. By deliberately crossing them, *Heyokas* questioned and defined the tribe's social boundaries. Their humour was not only frivolous fun, it was also sacred medicine, and Black Elk says that only those who had had a vision of the mythical 'Thunder Beings' could act as *Heyokas*. He says:

> You have noticed that the truth comes into this world with two faces. One is sad with suffering, and the other laughs; it is the same face, laughing or weeping. When people are already in despair the laughing face is better for them; and when they feel too good and are too sure of being safe, maybe the weeping face is better for them to see. And so I think this is what the Heyoka Ceremony is for.

He tells a delightful story of two comically painted *Heyokas* staring in terror at a small puddle of water, refusing to cross it as if it were some raging torrent. With clown-like exaggeration, one takes his bow and gingerly lays it flat across the puddle, as if measuring the depth. He retrieves the bow and places it upright against himself. The watermark seems to suggest that the puddle is dangerously deep and the water will come up to his neck! With a great show of courage, he plunges into the shallow puddle, fighting wildly as if drowning. His comrade plunges in to save him – and the bystanders enjoy the ridiculous spectacle. After a day of such fun, Black Elk remarks, everybody felt a great deal better:

> They were able now to see the greenness of the world, the wideness of the sacred day, the colours of the earth, and to set these in their minds.

THE SUN DANCE

At the centre of all aspects of Native American life was a profound sense of *spirit*. A pow-wow often climaxed with a 'Sun Dance', sometimes called the 'Dance of World and Life

Renewal', the 'Dance Watching The Sun', or the 'Thirst Dance'. This sacred ceremony connected the dancers and the whole tribe to Great Spirit. It was a dance of courage and sacrifice, a powerful spiritual ritual in which every element carried deep symbolic significance. It united the tribes and was a time for renewal and purification. It is still practised in modern forms to this day.

In preparation, the women cleared a sacred circle. A tree was erected in the centre, which symbolically connected Mother Earth and Father Sky. The male participants would have been purified in the Sweat Lodge (*see chapter 5*), and have undertaken a three-day fast. A man who had not danced the Sun Dance before had to have an experienced sponsor to testify to his worthiness. The initiate would have been prepared spiritually for this great test of his courage, endurance, and self-sacrifice.

When the time came, the dancer's pectoral tissues were ceremonially pierced through with a cherrywood spike, and connected by a thong to the Sun Dance Tree in the centre of the circle. He would now dance, without stopping, for four days and four nights, in recognition of the four sacred directions. To fall was a great disgrace to his sponsor and a bad omen for the whole tribe. He would on no account stop dancing, even as the movements of his body eventually ripped the cherrywood spike through the skin of his chest.

The Sun Dance was banned by the US Government, who deemed it to be a form of self-torture. But this was never a machismo ritual of self-aggrandisement. The pain was endured as a form of self-sacrifice. Men had the chance to show their willingness to suffer in order to protect the whole tribe, as women suffer for all when they give birth. Men could share their blood with the Earth, as a woman does in menstruation. In many tribes, a man who had not danced the Sun Dance had not shown himself to be ready to marry a woman.

The Sun Dancers believed that by suffering willingly, the fear of suffering could be overcome. While the men danced, the women may have cut small pieces of flesh from their forearms, to honour the dancers and share in the ceremony. The men blew whistles made of an eagle's wing-bone and decorated with eagle plumes. These whistles made the sound of an eagle's cry. The eagle is a very sacred bird for the Native Americans. It can fly very high, and has great powers of vision. As the whistles blew, it would have been as if the eagle was present. It would have been as if the dancers had become eagles, flying up to Great Spirit.

The drums, the fasting, the dancing, the sacredness of the occasion – all contributed to the spiritual experiences and visions of the participants. These visions may have brought *medicine* powers to a dancer, or a gift of prophecy. Sitting Bull foresaw, in a vision, his great victory against Custer at the Little Big Horn, after having danced looking at the sun for eight days!

This ceremony honours Grandfather Sun who loves Mother Earth, bringing Life to all with his light and warmth. It brings renewal – just as day follows night and summer follows winter. The dancers greet the new sun of each day, holding their eagle feathers out to catch the first rays; purifying themselves by the ritual movements of their bodies, as they ecstatically dance and sing:

> Here am I,
> behold me.
> I am the sun,
> behold me.

LAKOTA SUN-RISE GREETING SONG

THE 'OLD WAYS'

The Spirit of the Thunderbird
flies to all four corners of the Earth
and brings the people back
to the natural way of life,
not through religion
or a Native American way,
but through the 'Old Way',
that once belonged to all humans.

WA'NA'NEE'CHE'

The Sioux tell of how, in the old days, the Sacred Buffalo stood on four legs, whereas in our own times it totters unsteadily on just one. This image echoes the myth of the 'fall' of humankind, from a 'Golden Age' when all was in perfect balance, to our present state of disharmony. We hear similar stories from ancient cultures all over the world: the Vedic Hindus of India call our age the *Kali Yuga* – the Age of Darkness; the Ancient Greeks called it the Age of Iron; the Mayans called it the Last Sun. In the Golden Age, the Utopia of our ancestors, the 'Sacred Circle of Life' was unbroken. Medicine People could regularly perform great wonders;

the communication between the physical world and the spiritual world was clear and easy; people lived in 'the "Old Ways"' – in harmony with Mother Earth, and respecting all life.

According to our modern, linear, 'myth of progress', once we were primitives like the Native Americans and other ancient peoples; now we are sophisticated and civilized and 'better'. But, for the cultures of the world with memories of the 'Old Ways', rather than progressing to something 'better', we have 'fallen', and now live in an Age of Darkness, a sad time of separation from *spirit* and disconnection from the simple, natural harmony of life.

The Sioux Medicine Man, Lame Deer, says '...the Indian Religions are all somehow part of the same belief, the same mystery.' This common spirituality is an echo of the 'Old Ways', an echo also heard by Aborigines, Africans, Asians and other primal peoples. Their traditions are also somehow part of 'the same belief, the same mystery'. In fact, the further back a culture reaches into its ancestral memories, the more clearly it expresses a common approach to life. This ancient spirituality is not a dead religious tradition. It is an echo of a 'Golden' time; a memory. And now that these old cultures have all but been destroyed, it is an echo of an echo – a memory of a memory.

Whether or not this Golden Age was an actual time in history is unimportant. What matters is that it is mythically true – that the story carries power and resonance. The modern world is lost, because it has lost its memories of the 'Old Ways'. It no longer understands the spiritual dimension of life. According to the myths of the Primal Peoples, however, time moves in a circle, not in a straight line, and this Age of Darkness will pass, returning to a new Golden Age. Perhaps it is the memories of the 'Old Ways', held by the ancient peoples of the world, that

A VISION OF LIVING SPIRIT

In many ways it is misleading to see Native American Spirituality as a religious tradition. This Spirituality is not a set of dogmas demanding blind faith, or a moral code of rules and regulations that must be obeyed. The 'Old Ways' are a 'Way', just as flowing with *Tao* is a 'Way' for Taoists, or living one's *Dharma* is a 'Way' for Buddhists. They are a way of coming into natural harmony with life, and living from this centre of balance. In this state, which the Native Americans call 'Walking the Good Red Road', a person intuitively knows how to act and what is to be done.

The spirituality of the indigenous peoples of Turtle Island was rooted in their immediate experience of Nature, not in theoretical beliefs. There were no holy scriptures, seen as divine revelations. Great Spirit revealed itself each day, in the miracles of natural life and the visions of the people. Although there were special Medicine People with highly developed spiritual gifts, these were not like priests, passing on second-hand inspiration to a passive following. Each member of the tribe was encouraged, indeed sometimes required, to nurture their own direct connection to the unseen world through their relationship with Nature, through sacred ceremonies and by seeking visions (*see chapter 6*).

Through Native American eyes, the world is brimming with life. Every element of creation expresses the Creator, and every thing is alive in its own way. It is not just we 'two-leggeds' that have *spirit*, but also animals and plants – and even rocks, rivers and rainbows. The Creator created human beings last of all, by combining elements found in all the other forms of life. Thus humans find their place at the bottom of the Totem Pole, serving all other beings. Unlike minerals, plants and animals, who instinctively know their nature, we 'two-leggeds' need to learn how to live 'in balance' by observing the other creatures around us (*see chapter 3*). For those who follow the 'Old Ways', Nature is our schoolroom and all creatures are our teachers. We are part of the natural world, and we contain all the natural world within us.

Native Americans observed Nature with scientific precision, and learned profound spiritual lessons from her. By studying the intricately connected threads of a spider's web, they understood that there is one 'web of life', within which everything is related. Nothing exists in isolation. They saw that the threads of the web are drawn out from within the spider's very being – just as the Creator creates the natural world from within himself, and we create our own worlds within our consciousness.

For the people of Turtle Island, spirituality was not a part of life, but informed all of life. In no Native American language is there a single term that can be translated as 'religion', because all acts are seen as religious acts. Likewise, Native Americans do not have the concept of 'art'. The practical design and decorative embellishment of artefacts, dwellings, clothing and so forth, are spiritual symbols reflecting the Peoples' understanding of the harmony of life. The natural materials used in the designs were regarded as manifestations of sacred natural powers, or *energies*, giving the completed artefact its own *medicine* power through the synthesis of all these *energies* (*see chapter 4*). If an object has been created in 'spiritual balance', then it will bring balance to all who touch it.

From the perspective of our modern, 'logical' world-view, it is very easy to misunderstand this intuitive spirituality. It is easy to treat the Indigenous American perspective on life as a curious relic for anthropologists to pore over; full of bizarre stories and superstitions that, whilst they have a romantic fascination, we would never be so naive as to believe today.

What appears to be superstition, however, is often actually 'super-perception'. It can be modern man's lack of spiritual sophistication that makes indigenous people seem 'primitive' to him. A simple example of this is the often-reported concern of 'primitive' peoples that they will lose their souls when being photographed. From our technological perspective this seems ridiculous: amusing ignorance. But closer examination reveals that the indigenous people are experiencing a profounder reality.

Recently, a documentary-maker encountered such a reaction when filming the Kogi people in Columbia, South America, an isolated ancient culture still closely in touch with the 'Old Ways'. He pressed them to say more. The 'Mamas' – the Kogi Medicine People – explained that all objects are alive with a spiritual dimension, and that it is important that the physical and the spiritual be kept 'in balance'.

They explained that the camera that was being used to film them was 'out of balance' with the 'Whole of Life'. The resources used in its construction had been taken from Mother Earth in a way that was 'out of balance'. The motivation of the people who constructed the camera was 'out of balance' with *spirit*. The people using the camera were 'out of balance' with themselves. For these reasons, being around this technology made the Kogi feel 'out of balance' – as if their soul-energy was

being drained from them. Was it the Kogi that were being naive
and foolish, or the modern westerners, who had no perception
of this other spiritual dimension?

THE SACREDNESS OF ALL LIFE

For Native Americans, everything is sacred and alive with
spirit, so all activities are spiritual activities and must be
approached with an understanding of the unseen world. When
a woman from the plains decorates a robe with porcupine quills,
for example, she is not just making an aesthetically pleasing and
useful garment. She will fast and pray before beginning her
work, and as she works she will contemplate the brightly dyed
quills. She will have been initiated into an understanding of the
spiritual resonance between the porcupine and the sun, which
in turn resonates with the creative principle of life. The quills
she lays also become the sacred rays of the sun, now embodied
within the garment to concretely benefit the wearer.

The porcupine quills do not represent the power of the sun,
they actually embody the same *energy*. Likewise, Black Elk says
the act of hunting does not represent life's quest for ultimate
truth – it actually is this quest. A hunter is not just procuring
food. He is engaging in a deeply spiritual activity. He must
pray and purify himself. He must be observant and diligently
follow the tracks of his quarry. He must relate, in the unseen
world, to the animal he hunts, asking it to sacrifice itself for the
benefit of The People. A sacred harmony must be maintained at
all times if the hunt is to be successful.

When the rains don't come, the People may carry out a Rain
Dance. This will not 'cause' the rain to come, but it will re-
establish spiritual balance, so that the rain will come naturally.
Native Peoples do not pray to the dawn in the superstitious
belief that if they don't do this then the sun will not rise. It is

natural and in the harmony of life for the sun to rise and it is natural and in the harmony of life to greet the rising sun with prayer. If this sacred balance were to be broken, then who knows if a new day would dawn?

A 'tipi' decorated with an eagle motif, which embodies the power of 'Wakan Tanka'

SPIRIT, MIND AND BODY

This Earth-Walk is, above all, a sacred spiritual journey. The modern world has stripped away this meaning from life. We have fragmented reality. We see ourselves as isolated, separate beings, performing acts that have little importance beyond their successful physical completion. Wa'Na'Nee'Che' points out that even New Age thinking unconsciously relegates *spirit* in importance, when it defines a human as being made up of 'Mind, Body and Spirit'. For the Native American this should be 'Spirit, Mind and Body'. *Spirit* is primary. We are not human beings on a spiritual journey. We are spiritual beings on a human journey.

The part of each person that says 'I am' is a part of *spirit*. It is eternal and limitless. The mind functions as a link between spirit and body. The body is a shell. It is a part of Mother Earth, and it returns to her when we die. Our spirit is a part of the one Great Spirit, and if we are in balance when we die it may go through the doorway and return to the Whole. As Black Elk says, we will 'pass from this world of darkness into the other real world of light'.

The Plains Tribes called this entering the 'Sky Lodge', the name that they gave to the scaffolds they erected, upon which they placed their dead. Some tribes that lived by the sea buried their dead under a mound of shells, so that the deceased would hear clearly when to be reborn. The Pueblos buried their dead in the earth, so that they could journey to the under-world. Some tribes talk of passing to the 'Blue Road of Spirit'; others of 'Dropping the Robe', or going to the 'Other Side Camp'.

It is believed that immediately after death, the dead person remains in touch with their body for a few days. Sometimes they are confused and do not realise they are dead. After this, they have a little time to say their goodbyes, or do whatever they feel has to be done, before they return to the Sacred Light of Great Spirit. As in many other traditions – most famously the Tibetan Book of the Dead – the Medicine Person may use their powers in the unseen world to guide and assist the dead in this journey.

Wa'Na'Nee'Che' says that if a person is not 'in balance' when they die, they may be 'recycled' as another body which is appropriate for their *energy* – which may include becoming an animal or even a plant. A *spirit-energy* that continually fails to 're-balance' and becomes completely negative, may be sent to a place of such darkness that, through boredom, it goes into an eternal sleep. Some spirits are neither 'recycled' nor return to the Source, but hang around near the earth and are sometimes felt as a cold chill. Spirits that do reconnect to the Sacred Light may return as *energies*, and are felt as a warm glow. Like the inhabitants of the seen world, the inhabitants of the unseen world are of different sorts. They are not all wise, well-meaning and helpful!

The 'Old Ways' teach that there are *spirits* all around us; guiding us, helping us, and sometimes misleading and harming us. There are nature spirits of trees, plants, animals and so on, that other traditions call 'angels' or *devas*, as well as spirits of the ancestors and other disembodied ghosts. The Medicine Person, in particular, acts as an interface between the *spirit* world and the material world. It is only their connection with the great *energy* of *Wakan Tanka* that gives them the discrimination to tell these spirits apart.

WAKAN TANKA

Behind all of creation is an ultimate creative power, or God. The different nations call this supreme being by many names: for the Zuni it is the bisexual *A'wonawil'onas*; amongst the Amaha and Osage it is *Wakonda*; to the Pawnee it is *Tirawa*; to the Najaho it is the totality of all life, and therefore unknowable and may not be named! For the Sioux it is *Wakan Tanka*, usually translated as 'Great Spirit' or 'Great Mystery': he is both *Ate*, the Father of Creation, and *Tunkashila*, the

Grandfather – the non-manifest essence of life. All these translations, however, express *Wakan Tanka* as the name of something, as a noun. In the Lakota language *Wakan Tanka* is not a noun. It portrays something in movement, perhaps better translated as the 'Great Mysterious'.

The Sioux word *wakan* means much the same as the Iroquois word *orenda* and the Algonquin word *manitou*. *Wakan* is impossible to rigidly define. It means spiritual power or *energy*, and is often translated by the enigmatic term *medicine*. A Medicine Man is called *wicasa wakan*. Animals and plants have a particular *wakan*. Whiskey is *minne wakan* – *wakan* water – because it has the power to make men crazy. The world is full of *energies* and they all come from the one Great Energy. This Sioux concept is not far from certain doctrines of scientific materialism – the new religion of the modern world.

For mainstream Christianity, God exists outside his creation. For the Indigenous American, God expresses himself through his creation. If you want to see the face of your Creator, look around you. He/She/It is guiding and teaching you at every turn: here disguised as a tree, there as a bird, or a whirlwind, or a rainbow, or a river, or a mountain. To live in this awareness is to live synchronously in the physical and spiritual worlds. They are not separate. They coexist and interpenetrate each other.

SACRED LANGUAGE

For the Native Americans, a 'symbol' and the thing it represents share the same reality. A porcupine quill, the sun and *Wakan Tanka* all resonate together, just as different objects in a room all begin to resonate when a tuning fork is struck. For them, a name is not an arbitrary sign for the thing it represents; they share the same being. A name enfolds a reality within it like a hologram. Thus the name *Wakan Tanka* embodies Great Spirit.

Words have potency and force integral to their sound. They are sacred and magical. They are alive. They are born in the breath of the being that speaks them, and breath is the essential life force. The lungs are close to the heart and from them come words that carry ideas mysteriously upon the air from one awareness to another. Likewise, numbers are not seen as merely abstract symbols to count with. They contain the spiritual secrets of the Universe. Each number has a *spirit*, its own quality, which is a doorway into understanding the nature of Creation.

Unlike European languages which centre around nouns, most Native American languages are dominated by sophisticated verbs. Some Algonquin verbs, for example, have over one thousand endings! These languages portray a world of flux and change. 'Things' are like temporary whirlpools in a flowing river of constant movement. Names, like the objects they represent, are not fixed. An animal's name may vary from season to season as its coat or plumage changes. A person's name may alter as they progress through the initiations of their life. It is said that a man's life flows from his name like a river from its source.

Objects exist only through their relationships with each other. Definitions are not rigidly held, but kept open-ended – like the sacred circle of the Blackfoot, which is always left partly open to allow in the unexpected, or honour a forgotten *spirit*. Unlike western 'logical' thinking, with its mutually exclusive dichotomies, Native American thought stresses inter-relatedness across categories – placing everything within the context of the 'Whole'. For the logical mind, for example, something is either a chair or it is not a chair. But in a world seen in constant flux, a chair is a tree on its way to becoming broken bits of firewood!

The people of Turtle Island did not understand linear time as the modern world does. Many Native American languages do not have past and future tenses, but portray a perennial 'now'. The Hopi talk of things which are 'manifest' to the senses and things which are 'manifesting'. The future is seen as existing now, as an idea in the mind. Myths are not stories from the past, but exist eternally out of time, and are brought to life in the present as they are told.

THE STATE OF KNOWING

Native American languages often make clear in their verbal forms whether the speaker is talking from their own experience or relating someone else's. In the modern world, if we wish to add weight to what we have to say, we quote an external authority. For a Native American, direct personal experience is the highest authority that can be appealed to.

Knowledge is not perceived as being made up of facts that you can accumulate – like money in the bank. Rather, it is a *spirit* with which you must enter into a relationship – like a good friend. Knowledge exists independently of the knower. It cannot be 'forgotten and lost'. When certain songs are forgotten, with the death of a singer for example, they may come to someone else, quite independently, so that they may be sung again. A relationship with the *spirit* of a particular piece of knowledge comes with the responsibility to use it wisely, so that harmony may be maintained. Someone may not act on their knowledge unless authorized to do so by the spirit of that knowledge, or by someone else who has been so authorized.

For Native Americans, knowledge is not something that can be acquired passively, like facts learnt by rote in a schoolroom. Knowledge can only be acquired through experience; it is not information, it is a state of knowing. Perhaps it is because of this different understanding of the world that the people of Turtle Island did not develop sophisticated written language.

To set something down for all time would be to kill it – to pass
on the facts but not the 'knowing'.

LEARNING BY HEART

The Native Americans employed only rudimentary picture writing, on rocks, birch bark, wood panels, wampum belts and so on. Their knowledge and wisdom was 'learned by heart' and passed down through the generations by conveyed experience. If they had possessed great books containing their wisdom, maybe the European Invaders would have held them in higher esteem. The written word is seen as a sign of civilization, and oral cultures are often seen as having had nothing worth writing down!

It is said that writing preserves a thought for all time, while an oral tradition becomes distorted by constant retelling. But this mutability is in fact its great strength. Within an oral tradition, each generation contributes their experience to the telling of the truth. It is this ability to subtly adapt and change, in response to a changing world, that keeps the true essence of the tradition alive and relevant.

Spoken communication involves so much more than words. Great truths must be told in such a way that they 'hit' you emotionally. The animated story-teller can do this in a way with which the written word cannot compete – think of lines of Shakespeare that sound dry and dusty on the page, but come to life in the hands of a great actor.

As you read these words before you on the page, you cannot hear the tone of voice with which I would speak them to you, if you were in my presence. You cannot see my gestures and facial expressions. There is a gulf of space and time between my expression of these thoughts and your reception of them. Much of what I wish to encode, for you to decipher,

34

cannot be held within these symbols. I cannot address you in the way I would if I could sense your present mood, or knew your personal interests and misgivings – and you cannot 'feel' my presence and intention as clearly as if I were before your eyes.

Unlike books, which are often read once and then become a source of reference, unwritten wisdom must be fully ingested by the whole being. The stories that make up the world-vision of the tribe must be told and retold so that they can be felt and lived. As the contemporary American poet, Robert Bly, says when he recites poetry to the beat of his drum: 'The first time you hear a poem it gets as far as your neck. You need to hear it again if you want it to reach you in your guts!' This is why it is the oral traditions of the world that have kept alive the memories of the 'Old Ways' more than the sophisticated 'religions': 'The letter killeth – the Spirit giveth life'!

EXERCISE: 'THE WEB OF LIFE'

Here is a simple suggestion to help you move beyond the understanding of these written words, into the world of your own direct experience. Find for yourself a beautiful spot in nature, a place where you can be alone with the powers of the natural world, somewhere that has a special feeling with which you resonate.

Find your 'place to be', by walking clockwise in a circle until a particular spot seems to call to you. Mark it with a stone and continue walking. If the same spot calls to you again, this is your place in the circle. Every place on Mother Earth has a particular *energy*, and this is the place for you to sit today. Remain still, and let the agitated thoughts in your mind settle down – like dirt settling in a muddy puddle when the water is no longer disturbed. Look around you. Take in the *spirit* of this place – its unique character. Let yourself come into harmony with it.

Look at the sky above you. Watch the clouds passing, like your thoughts and feelings passing across the open sky of your awareness. Feel the ever-present heat of the sun, like the constant love of Great Spirit bringing life to Mother Earth. Look at all the life around you – the coming into being and the passing away. Become aware of more than your sense of sight, which often dominates the other senses in our modern world. You can only look in one direction, but you can hear all around; you can smell what is close to you; you can feel what is touching you. Open up all your five senses to the seen world around you, and your inner, spiritual sense to the unseen world that permeates it. Be fully in this place with all your being – Spirit, mind and body.

Breathe in the air that surrounds you. This is the same air that is breathed by all other human beings and all animals. It connects you to them by invisible threads. Feel the wind on your face – the spirits of the four winds, north, south, east and west, are the sons of Great Spirit. Which of these spirits is with you today? Like Great Spirit they pass unseen though the world, moving and shaping it. Listen to the sound of the wind in the trees. In the language of the Mic Maq people of Turtle Island, the trees are given names according to the different sounds the wind makes when it rustles their leaves in the autumn.

Be attentive to the wordless teachings of Nature. Sense your place in the great Web of Life. Reach out with your *spirit* to the living world that sustains you. Transcend your separate identity and allow a 'knowing' of the 'Whole'. As Black Elk says:

> Peace comes within the souls of men when they realise their
> relationship, their oneness, with the universe and all its powers,
> and when they realise that at the centre of the Universe dwells

Wakan Tanka, and that this centre is really everywhere, it is within each of us.

Open your heart to the Great Mystery of life that may be appreciated, but never solved.

'TO ALL OUR RELATIONS'

In the beginning of all things,
wisdom and knowledge were with the animals;
for 'Tirawa', the One Above,
did not speak directly to man.
He sent certain animals to tell man
that he showed himself through the beasts,
and that from them,
and from the stars and the sun and the moon,
man should learn.
Tirawa spoke to man through his works.

CHIEF LETAKOTYS – LESA PAWNEE

There is a saying used by many Native Americans when they are finishing a prayer, or a ceremony, or a serious talk. This saying is spoken in many different languages and dialects. In the Lakota language of the Sioux it is *mitakuye oyasin*, meaning 'to all our relations', or 'we are all related'. It reminds us that we two-leggeds share one Creator with the four-leggeds, the winged ones, the crawling people, the plants and 'standing people', or trees – even the 'stone people', the rocks and minerals. We are all one family. We are all of the earth and all made living by the love of Great Spirit. We are all part of one Circle of Life and our individual well-being relies on the health of the Whole.

The people of Turtle Island respected Nature. Animals and plants were gifts from Great Spirit, to be received with gratitude. They had given themselves up to become a source of food, clothing or shelter for the People, and this generosity deserved to be honoured. When collecting herbs, for example, the people of Turtle Island would first ask permission from the 'chief' *spirit* of the herb, the largest herb of that type in the area. If the request to pick the herb was denied, they would move on. If it was allowed, they would always leave the first seven herbs they came to, so that the herb would continue to flourish and be available for the next seven generations of their tribe.

The European invaders forgot this ancient wisdom. For them, nature was to be tamed and used, like the once wild animals now herded subserviently in their fields. The further 'civilization' has 'progressed', the further it has moved away from nature. Today we kill millions of animals every day, without according them honour or dignity. We do not think of them as a gift to us, nor that they are sacrificing themselves for our benefit. The truth is, we do not think of them at all. To the people of Turtle Island, the White Man was deaf to the harmonies of nature, because he no longer understood her language. This is why he was so disrespectful and destructive.

THE LANGUAGE OF NATURE

Some modern gardeners, however, have noticed that plants that are talked to and 'loved', flourish much better than plants that are not shown this care and respect. This is often seen as a strange and quirky belief, but to the people of Turtle Island, it was an obvious truth. Humans have often said, 'If only the animals could talk'. Could it be that the animals are saying, 'If only the two-leggeds would listen'! And not only the animals, but the birds and the trees, the rocks, the clouds, the lightning – the whole of Nature.

Medicine People say that plants 'talk' with colours, and animals with pictures, both of which may be seen with the inner eye of *spirit*. Occasionally they may even use words! Have you ever been walking alone in a forest, or some other wild place, and turned suddenly to see who is calling you? There is no one there but the trees. Could it have been the 'Standing People' – Grandfather and Grandmother Tree – calling you quietly in the wind? Or have you ever sat by a babbling brook and listened with your inner ear to the voices and music within the rushing ringing of the water? Could it be the water spirits singing to you?

To understand the language of Nature we have to enter into a different type of awareness, an awareness that is poetic, that delights in the senses – smell, sound, vision, taste and touch; that is intuitive and magical; that is respectful and observant. This 'animistic' awareness is often called 'primitive'. It comes naturally to children, and most people have faint memories of the magical world they inhabited in their early childhood. Is this an infantile stage that we have grown out of and which 'primitives' have been unable to transcend? Or, rather, have we abandoned our natural knowing, so that we may survive in our dead, harsh, 'grown-up' reality?

For the People of Turtle Island, everything was alive, and all forms of life were seen as 'our relations'. They believed that the Creator created humans last by combining all other life forms, therefore everything in Nature has something to teach us, if we are prepared to listen with the ear of our heart to the wordless language of *spirit* – a language which we all encounter, in one of its forms, in the strange symbolic events of our dreams (*see chapter 6*).

Medicine People must earn the right to the knowledge which Nature can reveal to them. If they petition with humility, a plant spirit may 'take pity on them', and reveal to them the medicine power of certain herbs; or an animal may become a *totem*, or Spirit Guide, imparting its particular wisdom. A Medicine Person who has built up a relationship with a particular herb, tree, animal, or rock, can call on that *energy* to assist them in their life and in their *medicine* work.

THE LESSONS OF NATURE

By observing the nature of the animals – their brothers and sisters the 'Four-Leggeds' – the people of Turtle Island learned how to walk the 'Good Red Road' of human life. The gentle deer taught them sensitivity; the loyal dog showed them the value of service and dedication; the snake that shed its skin spoke of the power of rebirth and transformation; the wily coyote imparted the gift of cunning; the humble ant displayed the power of patience and perseverance. In this way all the animals taught the People the wisdom of Great Spirit. Indeed, the people of the woodlands say that long ago the animals came in a special form, and married human beings to pass on to them their different qualities.

The trees – the Standing People – were also seen as brothers and sisters. Trees provide oxygen for all to breathe. Their branches are home to the Winged Ones, their roots are home to the smaller Four-Leggeds, and they give shelter to others under their branches. The People of Turtle Island honoured the Standing People for their generosity. If a tree would not let go of its fruit, they would not take it. If they were gathering nuts, they would only take a little from each tree so that plenty were left for the other creatures.

The Native Americans did not see Nature as a competitive

battle where only the fittest survive. This bleak vision is a reflection of the cultural values of European societies. To the People of Turtle Island, nature was a co-operative web of mutually beneficial alliances: when a bee takes nectar from a flower, it also picks up pollen to pass on to the next flower it visits, thereby helping the flower pollinate. In their relationship with nature, Indigenous Americans honoured this harmony of 'give and take' and lived within it.

SACRED LANDSCAPE

It was not only the animals and plants that were seen as sacred, but also the landscape they all shared. The Pawnee say: 'All things speak of Tirawa' – the Creator who shaped the land and gives it its every contour. Each hill tells a sacred story and holds a particular *spirit* or *energy*. Each valley is part of the body of Mother Earth.

When a believer sees a temple they do not perceive 'a building', but a 'House of God', with all its conscious and unconscious associations. In the same way, the people of Turtle Island did not perceive 'a landscape', but saw their spirituality and history embodied within the land. In 1854, speaking to the Governor of Washington, the Dwamish Chief Seattle said:

Every part of this soil is sacred in the estimation of my people. Every hillside, every valley, every plain and grove, has been hallowed by some sad or happy event in days long vanished. The very dust on which you now stand responds more lovingly to their footsteps than to yours, because it is rich with the blood of our ancestors and our bare feet are conscious of the sympathetic touch. Even the little children who lived here and rejoiced here for a brief season will love these somber solitudes and at eventide they greet shadowy returning spirits.

On visiting the plains at the time when the railroad was first cutting across these vast expanses, Henry James mused in *The American Scene*:

> If I were one of these painted savages you have dispossessed, beauty and charm for me would be in the solitude you have ravaged; and I should owe you my grudge for every disfigurement and every violence, for every wound with which you have caused the face of the land to bleed.

For the people of Turtle Island, nature was a great green cathedral, filled with the holy presence of God and all His gifts: the rivers which gave them water; the plants which fed and healed them; the animals whose hides clothed and sheltered them; the sacred places where they received visions and illumination. The greatest temples built by man will one day erode and fall, but the sacred caves and mountain tops will always endure.

POWER POINTS

All Native American land is considered to hold spiritual power and inspiration, but some spots are regarded as special 'power points' – places where lines of *energy* come together. These have been made sacred by being used for ceremonies. It is believed that the Stone People – the rocks – have recorded all the thoughts and actions that have been performed there, building up a reservoir of spiritual *energy*.

Such places are found all over the world. On Turtle Island there are the 'standing stones', 'rocking stones' and 'stone chambers' of New England; across the Mid-West there are the 'sacred mounds', like the Great Serpent Mound in Ohio, and the upper plains have the 'Medicine Wheels', the astrologically aligned stone circles. There are sacred springs which embody the spiritual power of water; caves that contain the power of earth; mountain tops which hold the power of air. In Kansas there is the sacred Mulberry cave and the Lyons Serpent: a 160 foot-long, snake-like form carved into the earth, and Penokee Man: small rocks laid out to form the shape of a giant man.

In Wyoming there is the Big Horn Medicine Wheel. Placed on the shoulder of a mountain in the Big Horn range, nearly 9,600 feet high, this is a stone circle some 90 feet in diameter. It has a central rock cairn which is 12 feet across and 2 feet high, from which radiate 28 spokes of smaller stones. This cairn is aligned with the summer solstice sun as it dawns and sets. It also aligns with the rising of the star of Aldebaran in the constellation of Taurus, the star Rigel in the constellation of Orion and the star Sirius in the constellation of Canis Major. These stars rise 28 days apart – one day for each of the 28 spokes of the Medicine Wheel. Similarly, precise stellar alignments are found in many other Native American Power Places. This was a culture that understood the movements of the heavens and their relationship with the earth.

The people of Turtle Island constructed 'Medicine Wheels' to focus and direct the *energies* of the earth and stars. Here they honoured the Four Directions of the land: East, West, North and South – which also embodied the Four Elements which combine to make up all Life: Air, Water, Fire and Earth – and the Four Races: Red, Yellow, Black and White – and the Four Parts of a human being: Spiritual, Mental, Emotional and Physical – and the Four Ages of a lifetime: Childhood, Youth, Maturity and Old Age – and the Four Seasons of a year: Spring, Summer, Autumn and Winter. Above is Father Sky and below is Mother Earth, and at the centre is each individual. These were the Sacred Seven Directions, sometimes called the 'Seven

Arrows'. All of Life is contained within the circle of the Medicine Wheel.

Black Elk says:

> Everything an Indian does is in a circle, and that is because the Power of the World works in circles, and everything tries to be round ... The sky is round and I have heard that the earth is round like a ball and so are all the stars. The wind, in its power, whirls. Birds make their nests in circles, for theirs is the same religion as ours. The sun comes forth and goes down again in a circle. The moon does the same, and both are round. Even the seasons form a great circle in their changing, and always come back again to where they were. The life of a man is a circle from childhood to childhood, and so it is in everything where power moves.

THE USE OF HERBS

In all Native American Sacred Ceremonies, the powers of the land, the animals, the plants, and all the forms of Nature are respected and evoked. To give a fuller and more 'rounded' picture of this intimate relationship with Nature, the final pages of this chapter explore in some detail one specific aspect of Native American knowledge – the use of sacred herbs.

Herbs were known to have the power to spiritually purify and bring balance to those unhealthy in spirit, mind or body (*see chapter 5*). Not all the sacred uses of herbs have been revealed by the medicine people who know these secrets, but much has been made available for common knowledge. The healing powers of different plants were learnt by observing the animals, who would naturally seek out certain herbs when they were unwell; humans followed their instruction.

Medicine People, having the ability to see in the spirit world, can also perceive plants speaking to us in colour. The 'auras' of different plants are of different shades. People also have auras that can be seen as colour, and the right herb for the right job can sometimes be found by observing the colour in the aura of a sick person, and then finding the herb with the right colour in its aura to bring healing. Present-day Medicine People sometimes have jars of herbs marked with colours rather than names! They, of course, can see the colour directly, but their helpers or apprentices do not always have this ability. For those of us who do not have this gift, let us look at some of the qualities and properties of different herbs:

TOBACCO

Tobacco is *wakan*, it has *medicine* power; to Native Americans, it is one of the most sacred plants. Its large, broad, pointed leaves are from six to twelve inches long, and this is the part of the plant that is smoked or burned. A common name amongst Native Americans for a smoking mixture is *kinnikinnick*. This may refer to the herb *uva-ursi*, but is more often used for a combination of tobacco and other herbs, prepared for smoking.

Some tribes say tobacco was the first gift from the Creator. Others tell the story of a sacred woman who was pregnant with twin boys. One of these sons represents all that is good in human beings, and the other represents all that is bad. Even before they were born, these two boys fought and argued. When she was giving birth, the good son emerged normally from her womb, but the bad son was so competitive with his brother, and so anxious to be born, that he kicked and pushed his way through his mother's side, mortally wounding her. The Mother told the good son that The People would benefit from her passing on, and instructed him on how she was to be buried. This magical boy did as his Mother commanded and waited by her grave. After a few days, three plants grew up from her body. These were the three 'sister plants' that

sustain and nourish The People – corn, beans and squash – and from her forehead came the sacred plant, tobacco.

Because it emerged from her forehead, this herb brings clarity. It can transform negative energies into positive energies – it is like a telephone line to the spirit world. Tobacco is burnt, smoked or used as an offering to get the attention of the *energies*, or as a call for help. It could be a 'local call', calling on spirit guides or the spirits of a place. It could be a connection straight through to Great Spirit. An habitual smoker is like a child playing on the phone. The people they frivolously contact will soon become annoyed with their 'false calls' and cease to answer them, even when they are genuinely in need of help.

Whatever illness a Medicine Person is seeking to cure, tobacco will, in some way, be part of the cure! This seems so strange to those of us who are used to tobacco smoking being portrayed as a deadly and stupid habit. But the Native Americans did not abuse tobacco. The tobacco they smoked was pure and was not mixed with chemicals. Smoking was not a casual, unconscious activity in the way it is today. That is not to say that smoking was always ceremonial and never done for enjoyment. But whatever the situation, the herb was honoured for its sacred nature. To do otherwise would have been to dishonour this gift of Great Spirit.

For the primal peoples all of life was sacred. In the modern world we have increasingly stripped away the spiritual dimension from life – and we wonder why things no longer hold together. The modern catastrophe of tobacco abuse, and all its related illnesses, is an excellent example of this. The modern world has no respect for plant life. Tobacco has become a quick 'hit' – a mild form of stress release to be thoughtlessly ingested in the form of conveniently packaged cigarettes.

To the people of Turtle Island, tobacco was sacred. Tobacco was *medicine*! Every smoker knows its calming properties, and this is why it was traditionally used in the 'Peace Pipe' during council meetings, as well as for healing and cleansing. But a powerful medicine which is taken for the wrong reasons, or without due care, becomes a poison and can cause illness. From this perspective, if you use tobacco habitually to suppress unconscious discontent, rather than to open you up to the unseen world, it will become a curse, not a blessing. Native American wisdom teaches that tobacco has the power to connect you with the world of *Spirit* – but smoke it without reverence and it will put you in the spirit world for good!

SAGE

The second gift of Great Spirit was *pe ji ho ta*, or sage. Like the Native Americans, many other cultures associate this plant with wisdom. In fact, we talk in English of a wise person as a 'sage'. This plant has lots of pretty blue flowers and light white or greyish leaves. It is a perennial which flourishes easily. It was used by the people of Turtle Island as both a culinary and medicinal herb.

Sage, too, is *wakan*, and has powerful *medicine*. It is believed to be a protection against malevolent powers and is therefore used before beginning a ceremony to drive away any evil spirits. It is a powerful purifier and is used in 'smudging' and the ceremony of the Sweat Lodge (*see chapter 5*), as well as by those preparing for a Vision Quest (*see chapter 6*). It has the power to draw out 'bad energies' that afflict the body or the soul.

Sage is said to have the power to help problems of the stomach, colon, nasal passages, kidneys, liver, lungs, pores of the skin, bones, and sex organs. It is good for the hair and scalp, as well as for burns and grazes. It can be used as an antiseptic and eases allergies, colds and fevers. As a gargle, it is taken for a sore throat. It is used for its perfume in types of aromatherapy, and can be taken as a tea to calm the nerves, or used in bathing

for cleansing. Someone who had unwittingly touched a sacred object would take a sage bath. Sometimes a bunch of sage was also used as a towel, to dry the body.

CEDAR

Han Te Sha, or cedar, is said to be the third gift of the Creator. The cedar is a tall, stately, evergreen tree, seen all over the world. It has the look of nobility about it, and the wisdom that only comes with age. But whether in its mature form, or as a short shrub, the cedar is a strong plant which can nurture and protect. In the old days, cedar bark was used for parts of houses, clothing, canoes and other artefacts. Cedar boughs were put on tipis to ward off lightning. Both the boughs and the inner bark were used in ceremonies.

Cedar is of the same spiritual family as sage and sweetgrass. Its *medicine* is milder than sage, and stronger than sweetgrass. Combined with these other herbs it makes a powerful concoction, often used in the sacred 'smudging' ceremony (*see chapter 5*). Cedar leaves and inner bark may be burned on its own, especially to cleanse the air after sickness. It has a pleasant pungent odour.

Cedar fruit and leaves are boiled and the mixture taken internally for coughs, a mixture also given to horses for the same reason. For a head-cold, twigs are burned and inhaled. It is said that boiling cedar and then drinking and bathing in the water is a cure for Asiatic Cholera. Because it will grow amongst rocks, cedar is used in the purification ceremony of the Sweat Lodge, to honour the hot rocks used to produce steam (*see chapter 5*).

SWEETGRASS

Wah Chan Ga, or sweetgrass, is a perennial plant that grows in damp environments, like marshes, or near water. It is sometimes called 'Hair of the Mother' because its long, reed-like leaves are often braided before they are picked. This practice reminds us that all plants grow from Mother Earth and we should honour her. Sweetgrass is often burnt by shaving little bits of these braids off onto hot coals, or by lighting the end of the braid and waving it through the air, distributing the smoke through the environment.

Sweetgrass is mixed with its spiritual cousins, sage and cedar, for use in the Smudging Ceremony. In the Sweat Lodge it is used as a purifier. The Lakota peoples used it in all their ceremonies to call the good spirits, and send prayers to the Creator on the rising smoke. Sweetgrass is believed to carry the deep wisdom of the Earth. Its sweet aroma attracts positive spirits towards the person burning it. It is used in the morning to bring refreshment and, like cedar and sage, it pleasantly perfumes the air at any time.

EXERCISE: UNDERSTANDING THE LANGUAGE OF NATURE

This is a suggestion to take you into a deeper connection with the spirits of Nature. It is a continuation of the 'Web of Life' meditation at the end of chapter 2. As before, first find yourself a beautiful 'place to be' in Nature, and settle into an inner calm and centred stillness. You may wish to burn some of the herbs that have been discussed, to bring purification and clarity.

Is there something around you that seems to pull your attention towards it? It may be an animal or plant, a tree or a stone. Concentrate on this 'being' as a living spirit. Open your senses fully and embrace its nature. Relate to it in ways more intimate than words: feel it, listen to it, taste it, smell it. Consciously send out your love to it, honouring it as an expression of the Creator.

Suspend the doubts of your rational mind for a moment and

allow this living being – this animal or plant, tree or stone – to talk to you. But don't expect this other being to speak in English. It will speak its own language which you must translate. Close your eyes and 'listen' to what this being is saying to your sense of touch and smell. Let colours and pictures come into your mind. Allow the spirit of this being to enter into your imagination. Use the power of your intuition to understand and appreciate this communication.

When you feel it is time to move on, give thanks to this spirit-being, to the spirit of this place and to 'Great Spirit'. Affirm *mitakuye oyasin* – 'we are all related'. Wa'Na'Nee'Che' says:

> This reminds us that the Creator – love – made fertile all of life and brought forth all beings that have been created: The animals, birds, insects, plants, water, air, fire, earth, trees and human beings, are all brothers and sisters. We are all of the Earth and the Spirit that moves in all things gives all beings their different shapes, qualities, gifts and powers. We are all one. We are all connected within the Circle of Life. If a person can reach the necessary level of spirituality and life-force energy, they may freely communicate with all parts of creation, as well as with the Creator. Look around and see what the Creator has made and you will see the Creator.

MEDICINE TOOLS

For us Indians there is just the pipe,
the earth we sit on
and the open sky.
The spirit is everywhere...
That smoke from the peace pipe,
it goes straight up to the spirit world.
But this is a two-way thing.
Power flows down to us through that smoke,
through the pipe stem.
You feel that power as you hold your pipe;
it moves from the pipe right into your body.
It makes your hair stand up.
That pipe is not just a thing;
it is alive.

LAME DEER – SIOUX WICASA WAKAN

The Earth is our Mother and all living things are our relations – not in a romantic, poetic sense, but quite literally. Even according to Darwin's Theory of Evolution, if you could keep tracing back your ancestral tree, it would pass further and further into history – passing beyond your human ancestors to your animal ancestors – beyond your animal ancestors to simple plant life – and finally beyond plant life to the Earth herself. The Earth is literally your Great, Great ... Great Grandmother!

The Medicine Person knows they are related to all other forms of life – to the animals, plants and minerals which surround them. For the Native American, these other forms of Life embody spiritual qualities which are also latent within human beings. By fashioning Medicine Tools from the things of nature – fur, bone, crystals, skins, teeth, talons, shells, roots, herbs, feathers and so on – the Medicine Person is able to evoke the spirits of the beings from which the tool has been made, and discover within themselves the qualities these things represent.

A Medicine Drum, for example, is made of wood and animal skin. When playing this drum, a Medicine Person may call upon the assistance of the spirit of the tree from which its frame was constructed, and the spirit of the animal whose skin became the drumhead. A Medicine tool is any artefact that has *medicine*, or Spiritual Power, for the user. These artefacts can be used in ceremonies to call on the *energies*. They are seen as physical embodiments of spiritual realities, and help the Medicine Person focus their inner powers. In a sense, they are also teaching aids. They help the uninitiated, first to contact, and then to work with these subtle *energies*.

MEDICINE BUNDLES

A Medicine Person will keep these artefacts in a Medicine Bundle – a large piece of cloth or hide, securely tied with a thong, yarn or string. The contents of this bundle are sacred. They are like a 'scripture' – a tangible history and reminder of all the powers and wisdom of an individual or a tribe. These magical tools represent totem animals, and other allies in the natural world. In a medicine bundle you may find a stone, a crystal, a seed pod, the tail of an otter, a tobacco tie, an animal tooth, a string of beads and so forth.

A person may own, or share in, many different medicine bundles: personal medicine bundles; medicine bundles of the tribe; a Sun Dance bundle for the Sun Dance Ceremony; a vision bundle for seeking visions; a bundle for dreaming; a bundle for hunting; a bundle for protection in battle; perhaps a bundle created specially for their own use, for a specific purpose, by a powerful Medicine Person. Some bundles were passed from generation to generation, or from one guardian of the bundle to an appropriate successor.

Tribal bundles were often called the 'Grandmothers', so named because they carry the nourishment and nurturing power necessary for the continued well-being of The People. Each passing year added to the power of this *medicine*, and the power and protection it contained were common to all the tribe. A guardian of a tribal bundle would have had his or her own tipi, which was a centre of spiritual protection for the whole camp. For the People, these 'Grandmother Bundles' were 'living beings' and were protected by warrior chiefs and never left alone or un-cared for.

In contrast to the collective *medicine* of the 'Grandmothers', a personal bundle was a private matter. It was forbidden to touch or inquire about another person's medicine tools, and the penalty for stealing another's bundle was often death. To openly reveal all of one's medicine tools was regarded as unwise, for this could leave the owner open to sorcery and bad *medicine*. Some of these bundles were small and were worn as pouches around the neck. If a person were to 'drop their robe' – physically die – before passing on their bundle, it would be burnt, so that their spirit would have no strings to catch it in this world, and they would be free to move on.

MEDICINE PIPES

An important and highly sacred artefact, often found in a bundle, is a Medicine Pipe. A pipe is *wakan*. Smoking sacred tobacco, and other herbs in the pipe, makes the breath visible as smoke – and breath is the source of life. Smoke is taken into the body and then released, rising upwards to carry prayers to Great Spirit. Those who share a pipe acknowledge that they share the same breath. The inhalation and exhalation of smoke is the ebb and flow of all life.

In the same way that there are many medicine bundles for different purposes, so there are many different pipes. There are peace pipes and war pipes, sun dance pipes and marriage pipes, pipes shaped to represent particular totem animals, pipes of a specific tribe or clan, personal pipes and council pipes, ceremonial pipes and social pipes. The most popular material from which to carve the bowl is hard, rock-like catlinite, known as 'pipestone'. The stem is made from wood, sometimes cedar, or ash, or another wood with a soft pithy centre that will make an easy inner channel for the smoke to pass along.

The bundle containing the pipe and the other things used in a pipe ceremony, such as tobacco, red willow, *kinnicknick* and sweet grass, is called a pipe bag. When not in use, the stem and bowl are separated and wrapped individually. The owner of a tribal pipe bag is often called a 'pipe carrier' or 'pipeholder', and will have earned this privilege through initiation and instruction. This is a sacred responsibility and the pipe-carrier must be pure of heart to undertake pipe ceremonies.

The pipe is more than just an utensil. Like all *medicine* tools, it embodies a profound symbolism that encodes the wisdom of The People. The bowl represents the female aspect of Great Spirit – Mother Earth. The phallic-like stem represents the male – Father Sky. Bringing these together represents the

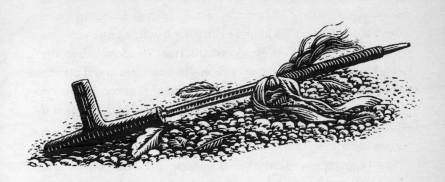

A sacred pipe

cosmic union that brings Life. The bowl represents the head and the stem the spine. The bowl contains the tobacco which is burnt to ash, representing all that changes. The stem signifies all that is absolute and unchanging. The bowl is the 'Wheel of Life' and the stem the still centre of the axial. When the smoker draws the smoke from the bowl through the stem, he remembers Great Mystery, which embraces both the ever-changing and the ever-constant.

The pipe is decorated with symbolism that is relevant and mythically numinous to the tribe or individual who uses it. Black Elk, the visionary Medicine Man of the Ogalala Sioux, describes his pipe as having four ribbons hanging from the stem – one for each of the four quarters of the universe. A black one for the west, where live the Thunder Beings who bring rain; a white one for the north, whence comes the white cleansing wind; a red one for the east, where the morning star lives to bring men wisdom, and from where rises the new light; and a yellow one for the south, whence comes the summer and the power of growth.

An Eagle feather also hangs from his pipe, to signify the One Spirit which unites these four quarters, and so that the thoughts of the smoker may rise high, as eagles do. There is bison hide on the mouthpiece, signifying Mother Earth, on whose breast all are suckled. Black Elk says, 'And because it means all this, and more than any man can understand, the pipe is holy.'

The pipe represents the 'four kingdoms'. The bowl made from earth is the mineral kingdom, the stem made from wood is the plant kingdom, the feathers and fur hung from the stem represent the animal kingdom, the maker of the pipe and the smoker represent the human kingdom. All four elements are also present. The tobacco and herbs that are smoked represent earth, fire burns these when the pipe is lit, air is sucked through the pipe to keep it alight, and water is represented by the spittle of the smoker.

Smoking the sacred pipe is central to all ceremonies. It is the connection between the two worlds of *spirit* and *matter* – its smoke a bridge between earth and sky. When not being smoked, it can be leant against a forked peg pressed into the ground, to become a portable altar – a object of meditation and contemplation. Like all Native American medicine, its purpose is practical, not theoretical. It is there to reveal directly to the user the secret wisdom it contains and to remind the People of the deeper realities of life. If the pipe should cease to be honoured, it is believed, the People will lose their centre and cease to be.

The pipe is used in council meetings and in Sweat Lodges, and it is the only thing a person takes with them when they go on a 'Vision Quest' (*see chapter 6*). Traditionally, a young man received his first pipe when he went on his first Vision Quest, aged between 13 and 14 years. A woman had to have passed her menopause before becoming a pipe bearer, as it was considered that, until this point, the power of her menstrual cycle was too strong and could upset the balance of the *medicine* of the pipe.

A tribal pipe carrier can be asked to smoke at births, deaths, marriages, contractual agreements, moon ceremonies and so on; to give thanks, offer prayers and to bring purification. The calling is comparable to that of a priest. A pipe carrier is the guardian of sacred tradition and is called to this office by a vision.

A PIPE CEREMONY

The pipe brings peace. But peace is not just seen as the resolution of conflict or war. Smoking the pipe brings balance, harmony, and inner well-being. A simple pipe ceremony may be as follows: each pinch of tobacco is blessed, and each of 'all our relations' is asked to enter the pipe in *spirit*, to be honoured and smoked. The pipe is packed a pinch at a time and each pinch carries a prayer, or petition. The pipe is offered to the seven directions – north, south, east and west, Mother Earth, Father Sky and Spirit within. This connects the smoker to all Creation.

The pipe is smoked with the bowl held in the left hand, because the left hand is closer to the heart than the right, and the heart is the centre of a human. The left is also the female hand. The right is the 'outer' hand, and holds the stem. Each smoker offers the pipe to Mother Earth and Father Sky, turning the stem clockwise once around the bowl and then passing it on. Clockwise is the solar way – the way of balance. It is used in most ceremonies. Some say the people of Turtle Island took up this practice after observing buffalo bulls moving clockwise in a large circle around their young, to keep them safe from predators. As the pipe is passed on, the smoker will say *mitakuye oyasin* – 'to all my relations'.

Every pinch of tobacco that is loaded into the bowl must be smoked. Each flake represents a sacred part of the whole of life, and if it is not turned to smoke, the spirit will not be released. If the smoke is not taken into the body, there is no communion with the spirits of 'all our relations' and ancestors. To empty a partly smoked bowl dishonours the spirits that have been called to join the smoke, and they may not return to help the smoker again. As the fire consumes the separate flakes of tobacco, it is as if the multiplicity of things in the Universe are returning to the one primal unity of Great Spirit.

MYTHS OF THE PIPE

'Duck' brought the pipe to the Arapahoe tribe. Thunder brought the pipe to the Blackfoot. The Cippewa tell how Great Spirit, weary of long and bloody tribal wars, made a gift of the pipe to bring peace to The People. Buffalo Calf Woman brought to the Sioux the seven Ceremonies: the Sweat Lodge, Crying for a Vision, Keeping of the Soul, the ritual of Throwing the Ball, the Naming of Relations, Preparing for Womanhood and the Sun Dance. Black Elk tells the following story of how She also brought the pipe to the Lakota peoples:

Two scouts were out looking for bison and saw a beautiful woman approaching. One of them was foolish and had bad thoughts about her, which he confided to his companion. The other recognised that this woman was sacred and told the foolish scout to throw his bad thoughts away. As she came nearer, they saw she was indeed a beautiful, long-haired young woman, dressed in fine white buckskin. She knew their thoughts and sang to them saying, 'You do not know me, but if you would act upon your thoughts come to me.' The foolish scout went up to her, but as he approached a white cloud came and covered them both. When the cloud passed, the young woman still stood there, but all that was left of the foolish young man was a skeleton covered with worms!

The beautiful young woman spoke, commanding the remaining scout to return home and tell the people that she was coming, and that they were to build for her a big tipi in the centre of the Nation. He returned to the people and soon she joined them, singing beautifully as she came. As she sang, a white cloud with a pleasing aroma issued from her mouth. She gave a pipe to the chief of the people. It had a bison carved upon it, to signify the Earth, that bears both humans and 'all their relations'. It had twelve eagle feathers hanging from it, to signify the sky and the twelve moons, and they were tied with a grass that never breaks.

'With this you shall multiply and be a good nation,' she said, 'nothing but good shall come from it.' Then singing all the while, she left the tipi. As the people watched her leave, she became a white bison snorting and galloping away. Black Elk said:

This they tell, and whether it happened or not I do not know; but if you think about it it is true.

Stories are also told of the origin of pipestone. Some say there was a great natural disaster many thousands of years ago, and all but a few two-leggeds perished. Nearly all the people of Turtle Island were crushed under the earth, or drowned in a tidal wave and mighty flood that covered the land. Over time, and under the pressure of the earth, the blood of these ancestors solidified to form the petrified blood-red rock now known as pipestone.

FEATHER MEDICINE

The natural objects used in *medicine* tools, like the sacred pipe, are selected for the particular spiritual qualities they embody. For example, a feather is a sort of antennae for a bird, through which it can sense minute shifts in wind current. In the same way, by analogue, a medicine person can use feathers in smudging and healing ceremonies, to sense and manipulate energy. Because feathers are linked to air and wind, and enable birds to fly, they are also used in blessings and prayers to carry messages up to Great Spirit.

In the popular imagination, no animal talisman is more associated with the Native American than the feather. Ancient figures in flowing feather head-dresses and warriors sporting brilliant single feathers are now archetypal images in world culture. But these feathers are more than decoration. They have spiritual power and significance. Feathers worn either singularly, or more commonly combined into a fan, are a mark of some physical or spiritual achievement. This applies especially to Eagle Feathers. The Eagle is traditionally regarded as the most noble and spiritual of all birds, and Eagle Feathers are often used in Native American dance costumes as a ceremonial head-dress. The wearer becomes identified with this great bird, who is in turn identified with the highest Spiritual Power.

Feathers were often used to decorate fetishes and shields, acting as magical protectors. Thomas Yellowtail, a contemporary Crow Medicine Man, tells how a young Crow warrior wore a Medicine Feather to Vietnam – 'just like the Medicine that warriors carried into battle in the old days.' Although many of his comrades were killed and a machine gun bullet left a bullet-hole in his shirt, he remained unharmed!

A Hopi dancer embodying an eagle spirit
(*Peter Newark's Western Americana*)

MEDICINE FEATHERS OF THE FOUR QUARTERS

A feather is consciously selected for a particular purpose, depending on its specific magical properties. This, in turn, depends on the spiritual qualities embodied by the bird from which it was taken. In Sweat Lodges, feathers from four birds are often placed on four poles in the four directions: an eagle feather in the east, an owl feather in the south, a raven feather in the west, and a hawk feather in the north. These feathers resonate with the symbolic qualities of the four quarters, creating a precisely orchestrated alchemy of energy that helps make a Sweat Lodge a powerful place of purification and prayer (*see chapter 5*).

EAGLE FEATHERS

Eagles see clearly and can fly to great heights. For these reasons, their feathers may be used to carry prayers up to Great Spirit. These feathers are ubiquitous in Native American culture. They are worn as a badge of honour for Medicine People, Chiefs and Warriors. *Wabun*, the Spirit Keeper of the East, is represented by a Golden Eagle. Its golden feathers represent the light of the dawn and the wisdom that everyday is a new beginning.

OWL FEATHERS

Although feared by some as 'The Bringer of Death', the Owl is also thought to teach wisdom, perception, discernment, and the ability to see through deception. Owls are powerful bringers of dreams and visions. Their *medicine* is thought to be so strong that their feathers should not be mixed with others, or used lightly or irresponsibly. It is said that wrapping Owl Medicine in a red cloth will contain its power and keep it separate from other energies. Some Native Americans will simply not touch an Owl feather. Much of its *medicine* is secret, because it relates to ancient feminine mysteries. If you want answers, conduct a ceremony using owl feathers – but be prepared for your life to be transformed by the answers you receive. Owl is the teacher of paradox and mystery; life and death; listening; the feminine; the dark; the unknown.

Nearly all Native American peoples have a legend about how the raven got its distinctive black colour. In these stories the bird starts as white, and is changed as a punishment for some wrong doing, or as the result of some danger. In most stories, Raven is depicted as changing colour whilst trying to help humanity in some way. To some, ravens are good omens. To others, they are bad omens. To some, they are the bringers of dark rain clouds and to others they are responsible for keeping them away. They are considered 'birds of the balance' between humanity and nature. Their feathers may be used to help achieve a more integrated relationship with the natural world.

HAWK FEATHERS

Like the eagle, the hawk is known for its clarity of vision and its ability to reach great heights during flight. For this reason it is called the 'Messenger of Spirit'. Red-tailed hawks are especially important to Native Americans. Pueblo peoples refer to them as 'red eagles'. Their feathers, like those of the eagle, are used in healing ceremonies. People of the south-west of America use their feathers to bring rain. Hawk *medicine* teaches adaptability, clear vision, far-sightedness, leadership, deliberation and optimism.

THE SPIRITUAL QUALITIES OF OTHER FEATHERS

The Loon is associated with the moon, and their feathers can bring creative inspiration and madness. Because they mate for life, they are also symbols of fidelity. The Condor is called the scavenger. Condor feathers can be used to remove negative energies. A Snow Goose feather can be used to bring stability and community. A Crow feather can confer magical powers. A Swan feather brings a gentle feminine energy. A brightly coloured Macaw feather can bring joy and wonder.

The Turkey is sometimes called 'the Earth Eagle' and 'the Giver of Gifts'. It provides on the physical plane, in the same way that the eagle provides on the spiritual plane. Turkey feathers can be used to increase material abundance. The tiny Hummingbird represents clarity and 'getting to the heart of things'. It is a 'doctoring bird'. Its feathers can be used to clear out old wounds and bring new light to old problems. It can 'sew up a wound' between people. It is a teacher of grace and tenacity.

The Flicker is a drummer. It plays on the limbs of dead trees, and similar objects, to bring out insects. The blood red colour of feathers from the red-shafted flicker has led them to be associated with War Spirits. Red feathers on prayer sticks are considered war offerings against either a human or a spiritual enemy. Flickers teach music, joy, nurturing, courage and protection.

EXERCISE: HOW TO USE FEATHERS AS MEDICINE TOOLS

It is not normally appropriate for non-native peoples to drape themselves with feathers, but there are many ways to benefit from their influence in daily life. A hawk or buzzard feather kept in the sunshield of a car will improve vision and give protection. Even feathers in a hat band, or as earrings, can be helpful if they are worn with a clear spiritual intention, rather than just cosmetically. Simply carrying a particular feather, or using it as a focus of contemplation, can bring the benefits of its specific qualities. If you need some spiritual insight, for example, you might meditate on an eagle feather. If you need some practical assistance, you may carry a turkey feather. The following exercises are simple ways to use Feather Medicine.

You may not have access to many of the more exotic feathers traditionally used by the people of Turtle Island, but this obstacle can easily be turned into an opportunity. Ask yourself which bird, indigenous to the area you inhabit, you feel drawn to. Maybe you will start noticing a certain bird song, or find a feather that attracts you. Perhaps a bird will come to you in a dream, or you will find a dead bird on the road or in the countryside. Whichever way your feathers come, just wash them gently in water. They generally don't decay as they have no fat on them. If the feather is split, take a smaller feather and glue it over the split. This will preserve its power, which may otherwise dissipate.

All birds, not just those listed above, have their own *medicine*. There may be folk traditions in your own area of the world, associating certain qualities with different birds. If you don't have access to this information, simply sit with your feathers, and ask yourself what are your own intuitive associations with this particular bird. Let the spirit of the bird rise up inside you and reveal itself. It will tell you what *medicine* the feather carries, and to what purpose it may be put.

BINDING A 'DREAM BUNDLE'

A 'Dream Bundle' is an aid to dreaming. It is a collection of feathers bound together with thread, yarn or cloth, and placed over the bedhead whilst sleeping. It can bring clear dreams or focus energy on some particular intent. Owls are night birds and are commonly linked to the dream world. Their feathers are often used in a 'Dream Bundle'. So are Hawk feathers, which bring 'messages from spirit'. The Dream Bundle becomes a sort of spiritual magnet which attracts the required *medicine* to the dreamer. Select a number of feathers that you feel will be appropriate for your bundle. Bind them together, whilst focusing on the medicine you wish the bundle to embody. When sleeping under the bundle you may like to keep a dream-diary as a record of the messages and experiences you receive.

OFFERINGS WITH FEATHERS

Whenever you take something from nature, it is good to leave an offering to honour the help you have received. There are many ways of making an offering, and many things that may be offered. The important element is your inner feeling of gratitude. Feathers can make a beautiful offering, perhaps lying them in a bush or tying them on a tree. These simple acts, when performed with 'intention', can help build an important inner connection with Nature. We often spend time asking for help. It is also important to say 'thank you' for all we have received.

HEALING AND PURIFICATION

The Earth, its life am I
Hozhoni, hozhoni
Its feet are my feet
Hozhoni, hozhoni
Its body is my body
Hozhoni, hozhoni
Its thoughts are my thought
Hozhoni, hozhoni
Its speech is my speech
Hozhoni, hozhoni

NAJAHO SWEATHOUSE SONG

The Najaho word *hozhoni* expresses 'harmony', 'peace', 'beauty', and 'balance'. For the Native Americans, life is like a great song, with each element in perfect harmony with every other, and it is when this natural balance is upset that illnesses, bad harvests, failure of the hunt, and other human misfortunes occur. European culture has belatedly discovered the truth of this in relation to the environment. We are now witnessing the fact that reckless interference with the eco-system leads to unforeseen and often catastrophic consequences. However, the notion of 'fundamental harmony' that the primal people possess goes much deeper than this. For them, the need for balance pertains to every area of life.

For an individual to be 'well', they must be in balance, both within themselves, and in relation to their society and all the natural world. Each individual is a part of the great Circle of Life. If they live as if they are separate from it, then disaster will inevitably follow – not as some form of retribution from a judgmental God, but because they are singing out of harmony with the Whole, and jarring clashes of disharmony will result.

All Native American rituals serve as opportunities to bring the participants into harmony with themselves, with their tribe and with all of life. The Pipe Ceremonies, the Sun Dance, Smudging, the Sweat Lodge, and so on, all 'purify' the participants by reaffirming for them their interconnectedness with each other and with their world. Every time a Native American says *mitakuye oyasin* – 'we are all related' – they acknowledge their place as an interconnecting part of the Circle of Life. The well-being of each individual depends on the well-being of all.

BREAKING TABOOS

Disharmony has its root in the 'unseen' world but shows itself in the 'seen' world. It may be traced to the breaking of a sacred tribal taboo. Taboos should not be dismissed as mere superstition. These customs and practices only seem arbitrary and meaningless when they are cut away from their spiritual context. All things in the lives of primal peoples have significance in the unseen world. Taboos often have practical importance – such as not picking the first herbs one finds in order to ensure the continuation of the species for future generations (*see Chapter 3*) – but they are also important spiritual statements. The person who breaks a taboo no longer understands its true meaning. Such a person is already out of balance with their own *spirit*, and all they touch will become out of balance.

When the first Christian missionaries came, many Native Americans presumed that they personally understood the truth of all they preached about the Bible and 'the right way to live'. To tell a lie about *spirit* was, to the Native people, unthinkable. It was to court untold disaster. Likewise, they were unable to comprehend the ability of the White Invaders to break their word. An agreement sealed with the sacred pipe was an agreement that must be respected. To do otherwise could not possibly be to anyone's advantage! The result of the lies of the White Man is the disharmony we see all around us today.

BAD SPIRITS

The unseen world is inhabited by many *spirits*, and these may be good or bad, engendering harmony or disharmony. In common with many Native Americans, Wa'Na'Nee'Che' talks of these as *energies*. This is probably a better term for the European mind to grasp than *spirit*, which can provoke ridiculous cultural stereotypes, such as ignorant savages propitiating bizarre non-existent ghosts.

The spirits must be appeased for the crops to grow, in the same way that the ground must be watered for the crops to grow. In a world-view that has not divorced *spirit* from Nature, these two statements speak of the same reality. Each element of Nature must be honoured and respected for the part it plays in Creation. Everything has a *spirit* or an *energy*. Energies that are out of balance are negative energies – bad or angry spirits – and can cause harm.

HEALTH AND ILLNESS

Energies may be manipulated for good or ill – to bring healing or, in malevolent witchcraft, to cause harm. The *medicine* used by a Native American Medicine Person is their ability to work with these energies to bring balance. They work in the unseen world, to restore harmony to the seen world. Even the use of herbs for healing, which may to the modern mind seem comparable to western medicine, is primarily a 'magical' act. A herb will heal because its *energy* will bring the patient back into balance (*see Chapter 3*). When diagnosing an illness, a medicine person looks into the unseen world to see where the sufferer is out of balance, and calls on the energies – through herbs, ritual, or what we might call counselling – to restore harmony and therefore health.

It is tempting to assume that modern medicine can 'explain' what the herb is actually doing chemically, and that the rest is superstitious nonsense. But this analysis completely misses the point. For a world-view that still sees Creation as an expression of *spirit*, it would be no surprise to discover that the healing energies of the herb physically manifest themselves as a chemical interaction with the patient's body. In this view, the chemicals make up the physical body of the *spirit* of the herb, and perfectly express its *medicine* power. While the modern view has focused on achieving an impressively detailed knowledge of the material world, this has been gained at the expense of ignoring the greater spiritual perspective.

As we have already explored, a person is spirit, mind and body. A disharmony of mind, such as worry or guilt, can express itself as disharmony of body, such as tension, headaches, ulcers or constant fatigue. Disharmony may manifest itself as simple feelings of unhappiness, or as the intense pain of a kidney stone. As everyone is unique and has their own place in the Circle of Life, so harmony is different for each individual, and the skill of a Medicine Person is to see into the unique predicament of a particular individual, and restore them to balance so that healing can naturally occur.

In modern society, one 'expert' treats the body and another the mind, while the spirit is the business of a completely separate group called 'priests'. To the Primal Peoples, this is complete craziness! The Medicine Person does not aim to cure the symptoms of an illness as a modern doctor might. Nor do they aim to treat the 'whole' person, as New Age practitioners often claim to do. Rather, they bring the person into balance with the natural harmony of life. This is a type of healing that can embrace death as something other than failure – because sometimes it is right to die. A good death is a natural part of the Cycle of Life.

Native Americans do not treat the body as if it were a car that you take to a mechanic to get fixed when it goes wrong. The body is an expression of *spirit*. Each individual is responsible for their health. Through tribal teachings they will have learnt that all their thoughts and actions, unimportant though they may seem, create ripples in their own being and in the world around them, like a pebble cast into a pond. It is not who a person is, or what happens to them, that creates disharmony. It is the responses they make to any given situation – the pebbles they choose to throw.

As a modern-day Native American Medicine Person, Wa'Na'Nee'Che' prefers to call himself a 'Spiritual Advisor'. This term conveys the essential role of the shaman, helping each individual meet the challenges of their own life in a way that puts them in harmony with their own spirit, their world, and the Great Mystery that embraces everything.

THE SWEAT LODGE

The 'Sweat Lodge', called *inipi* by the Lakota Sioux, is a ceremonial construction used for healing and balancing. In this small, dark enclosure, hot stones are covered in water, creating a steam bath. The Sweat Lodge is found in different forms all over Turtle Island. On the plains they were temporary erections made of willow poles covered in buffalo hide. Inthe Northeast, the poles were often covered in birch bark. In California, the Sweathouse was both a ceremonial centre and a dwelling place. In the far Northwest, they were sometimes made of cedar planks. The polar Inuit, often known as Eskimos, even had sweats inside their igloos!

The use of a Sweat Lodge for spiritual and physical purification was not only widespread in Turtle Island. They are also found all over the ancient world, for example, the savusauna of Finland, known to us simply as a 'sauna'. To most of us this means a pleasant experience at the local health suite. But there is an old Finnish saying that goes: 'In the sauna one must conduct oneself as one would in church'! This is a European memory of a time when spiritual and physical health were still seen as intimately connected.

The ancient Celts had Sweat Lodges made of sod and stone. In northern Russia they constructed steam bathhouses of wood, sometimes partially submerged in the ground, or even totally underground. Even today, the peasants use them for ritual, therapeutic treatments and social affairs. The ancient Japanese had ceremonial steam baths called mushi-buro. In Africa, steam purification is still widely practised. In 425 BC, Herodotus wrote of the sweat bath customs of the Scythians. Homer and others talk of laconia, the steam baths of the Ancient Greeks. These became the Roman balneum which, after the fall of Rome, were embraced in the Arabic

WHY SWEAT?

Sweating is a natural bodily function. If a human's sweat pores are blocked, they will die very quickly. The skin uses these pores to remove toxins from the body, which is why it is sometimes called 'The Third Kidney'. When we sweat, we literally burn up many bacterium that can't survive at these temperatures. The heat also stimulates the endocrine glands. The capillaries dilate and the heart pumps more blood. This flushes impurities out of the body's organs. Also, an excess of positive ions, often found in city air for example, causes tenseness and fatigue and is frequently linked to asthma, insomnia, heart attacks and allergies. Pouring water onto hot rocks releases an abundance of negative ions, counteracting these effects.

These are only the physical advantages of the sweat. The Sweat Lodge also has deep spiritual meaning, bringing balance and health to spirit, mind and body. It is a purification ritual used before the Vision Quest (*see Chapter 6*) and all other important spiritual undertakings. For some native peoples, it is performed daily as physical and spiritual hygiene. It is used to bring clarity to a specific problem, to call upon helpful spirits, to re-connect to Great Spirit.

The Sweat Lodge is a womb from which the participants are reborn to live more fully. The *Inipi* Lodge of the Plains Peoples is a dome, which seems to protrude from the ground, as if Mother Earth were pregnant. The participants enter as spiritual embryos, and emerge with the freshness of new-born babies. It is a sacred place – a place of prayer. Everything used in the Sweat Lodge comes from Mother Earth and reminds the participants of their interconnectedness with her.

Siwash Indians next to a sweat lodge, the frame formed
by Willow Poles (*Range/Bettmann/Underwood*)

THE FRAMEWORK OF RIBS

The process of building a Sweat Lodge is performed with a
sacred awareness, so that everything that happens within the
Lodge will bring balance and harmony. The frame is made of
willow saplings, which are straight and supple. When they are
cut, tobacco is offered in thanks. Every part of the process has
spiritual significance. When these poles are bent and tied
together at the top, the crossing poles form a square with four
sides, representing the sacred four directions. Cultivating a
reverent gratitude and an awareness of symbolic meaning, the
builders of the Lodge prepare themselves for a powerful ritual
experience, and the Lodge itself becomes imbued with positive
energies. Popping down to the sauna at the local health club

may be convenient, but we pay for our unwillingness to prepare ourselves by having the experience but missing out on its 'meaning'.

When the frame of the Lodge is complete, the poles connect to create what looks like a beehive, or an overturned basket. This roof is symbolic of the arch of the sky. In some traditions the poles are seen as 28 ribs, like the ribs of a woman; as well as those of the female bear and turtle which are both important totem animals. The number 28 also expresses the Lunar Cycle with its connection to female menstruation. Taking part in the sweat ritual was often compulsory for men, to help them connect to the female energies of Mother Earth. For women, who are considered to be naturally cleansed and connected to these energies by their monthly cycle, it was usually voluntary.

The willow is the representative of the plant life in the Sweat Lodge Ceremony. Black Elk tells us that the deciduous nature of the willow teaches us about the spiritual rebirth experienced in the Sweat Lodge. He says:

> In the fall their leaves die and return to earth, but in the spring they come to life again. So too men die but live again in the real world of Wakan Tanka, where there is nothing but the spirits of all things; and this true life we may know here on earth if we purify our bodies and mind, thus coming closer to Wakan Tanka who is all purity.

In the Seneca tradition the willow is the tree of love. It yields gracefully and is not easily broken. It is also a tree often found near streams and rivers, and therefore has a special relationship with water. Water is central to the Sweat Lodge Ceremony. It is poured onto the hot stones in the Lodge, rising up to Great Spirit as steam and returning to Mother Earth as the perspiration of the participants. It purifies and animates all life. Willow is also an important medicine tree. Willow bark is a traditional cure for headaches and other pains, which modern scientists have synthesized into acetylsalicylic acid – better known as 'aspirin'!

THE SKIN

The framework of ribs is then completely covered in buffalo hides or other skins, forming a small, totally sealed, dark space. This covering is the representative of the animal world in the Sweat Ceremony. Today, heavy blankets and quilts, or canvas and plastic, are often used instead. If the cover is the hide of a powerful animal like a bear, then that energy will be invited to come into the sweat. The bear reminds us of the cycles of life and death because it hibernates throughout the winter. The Iroquois are said to have used such Sweat Lodges to bring people back from the dead!

This covering is seen as the skin of a giant animal, and the poles are its ribs. The Lodge is now a living being, within whose body the participants are contained. To the Nez Perce, the Okanagan, the Colville, the Yakima and other tribes of the Pacific Northwest, the Lodge embodies the Spirit Chief who gave the animals their names. When you enter it, you enter something alive, and with mighty powers of transformation.

OUTSIDE THE LODGE

A small pit is dug at the centre of the Lodge, ready to receive the hot stones. The earth that is removed is used to make an 'altar' some five feet from the door of the Lodge. A branch representing the 'Tree of Life' is placed in the middle of this mound, and surrounded by small stones. Antlers, which will be used to move the hot stones within the Lodge, are placed around this altar, as is the sacred pipe. Individuals may place medicine objects here to be blessed – but no one may touch an object belonging to someone else.

'The One Who Pours The Water' within the Sweat Lodge will purify this whole area outside the Lodge, by 'smudging' it with sacred herbs like sage and sweetgrass to ensure the presence of positive energies (*see exercise later in this chapter*). With his helpers, he will chop wood and build a fire in a specially prepared fire pit nearby. 'The One Who Pours The Water' is comparable to a priest in this ritual; during all the preparations they will attempt to remain in a clear and aware state of mind. The 'stone tender' will stay outside the Lodge, heating the stones in the fire and passing them into the Lodge when summoned by 'The One Who Pours The Water'. All the stones that are heated will be used – except one. This one is left for the spirits to sweat with. It honours the spirits who have come to join in the ceremony.

THE STONE PEOPLE

Traditionally, the stones used in the ceremony are lava rocks that will not fragment when heated. Stones are our oldest living relatives. They were here long before people and the Native Americans often refer to them as 'elders'. In Lakota they are called *tunka* from *tunka-shila*, meaning 'grandfather'. They are regarded as the wisest of all things, and the Sweat Lodge is sometimes known as 'The Ceremony of the Stone People'. They can absorb illness, impurities and negativity in the same way that they can absorb heat. They carry ancient earth-records and release these memories as steam when water is poured upon them.

Lakota traditions say that Creation began by a great stone rising from the waters. In the Sweat Lodge, when the glowing hot stones are brought in, it is as if we are returning to the primal dawn of time. The Iroquois say that at one time people did not tell stories; then a great rock began to tell the tale of a boy called *Gah-gah* or *Crow* – and so began the tradition of story telling. The Lakota have the myth of *Stone Boy*, the child of a woman and a rock, who brings the first *Inipi* to the People.

The stones are always treated with reverence and respect. If one is dropped on its journey into the Lodge, it is usually put back into the fire outside and a new stone selected. The number of stones used will depend on 'The One Who Pours The Water', and the type of ceremony that is to be performed. There are many different ways of conducting the proceedings. In the sweats led by Wa'Na'Nee'Che', 28 stones are used: seven stones are brought in – representing the sacred seven directions – in four consecutive 'rounds' – representing the four sacred elements.

THE EXPERIENCE OF A SWEAT LODGE

When everything is prepared for the sweat, 'The One Who Pours The Water' often leads the participants in a sun-wise circle (clockwise) around the Lodge, whilst praying for a good sweat. Finally they are led into the dome itself, crawling on all fours through the low door, as if to enforce a sense of humility. As each person enters they affirm *mitakuye oyasin* – 'we are all related'. The participants crouch or sit on the earth in this small confined space. There may now be prayers and the sharing of the sacred pipe, before the hot rocks are brought in one at a time and placed in the central pit.

I will never forget the surge of panic I felt as the flap was pulled down during my first participation in a Sweat Lodge –

plunging me into utter darkness. It was like death, like being buried alive; the claustrophobic sensation of being pressed into a small space with a number of other people, with only the soft glow of the rocks; the feeling of magic and other presences as 'The One Who Pours The Water' began offering prayers and burning herbs on the hot stones; then the pouring of the water and the sudden rush of steaming heat, making my heart pound. I knew already that this would be a cathartic and initiatory experience.

It was reassuring to remember that I could call out *mitakuye oyasin* at any time, and the door would be opened to let me out. But I felt I was starting on a journey that it was important to complete. The steam rose from the hot stones, like the breath of the Creator. 'The One Who Pours the Water' gently tapped a drum and sang. It was, at the same time, a reverent but relaxed atmosphere. There was no room here for sanctimonious piety. We were all too close to the earth for that. Prayers calling the spirit helpers of the seven directions were interchanged with jokes and laughter to defuse any fear or discomfort.

After some time, 'The One Who Pours The Water' shouted *mitakuye oyasin* and the 'fire tender' outside the Lodge opened the flap, letting in a gush of cold air. This signalled the end of the 'first round'. Seven more glowing stones were brought in and added to the fire; antlers were used to place them in position. The door was once more sealed and water again poured onto the rocks, building up the heat in the Lodge.

The 'second round' was for healing, and 'The One Who Pours The Water' called in healing energies for purification and balance. He scattered red willow and osha on the stones, which flared and spat in the darkness like shooting stars, releasing a wonderful fragrance into the Lodge. After some time, the flap was opened again and welcome fresh air relieved the intense heat. The pitcher of water was passed around, to be drunk or sprinkled on parts of the body for healing. This was now *wakan* water, imbued with magical properties.

Before long, seven more hot stones were brought in. The 'third round' was for prayer and each participant in the Lodge offered up a personal appeal for guidance, or for a loved one, or for the healing of our earth, each concluding with 'we are all related'. Sometimes this is called the 'suffering' round, and often this is the hottest the Lodge gets. It can feel like you are cooking! This is the time to be aware of the hurts and wrongs that we have done to others, and to suffer alongside all those who are sick or in pain. As the door is opened at the end of this round, the steam escapes out, carrying these prayers up to Great Spirit.

Then another seven stones were carefully brought in, making 28 in all. The 'fourth round' was to give gratitude to the Creator and all the spirits for our experiences in the Sweat Lodge. Finally, the flap was opened for the last time and we began to file out into the cold fresh air. It was like leaving the house of darkness and emerging into the light; like being reborn from the womb of the Mother Earth herself – revitalized in spirit, mind and body; purified from the inside out; reconnected to ourselves, our world, each other and all of Creation. I under-stood more deeply the recurring refrain *mitakuye oyasin*.

'All our relations' are present in the Sweat Lodge. The circu-lar frame of the Lodge, like the Sacred Hoop of Life, contains all within it. The four elements are there: fire heats the stone which represents the earth element; water becomes steam which rep-resents the air element. The 'Two-Leggeds' are represented by the human participants; the 'Four-Leggeds' are represented by the hide skin and the antlers used to move the Stone People. The Winged Ones are represented by the feathers often hung to mark the sacred four directions, (*see Chapter 4*). The Standing People are represented by the willow poles, and the Plant

People by the herbs that are burnt and the tobacco smoked. Even the Crawling People are there, running over your feet in the darkness to escape the heat!

THE SWEAT LODGE TODAY

When the White Invaders first encountered the Sweat Lodge they were appalled. It is hard to conceive that at this time most Europeans regarded even bathing as strange and unhealthy! Whether it was because of this lack of understanding of hygiene, or because of their desire to destroy the native way of life, the White Man harshly persecuted the practice of ceremonial sweating. In 1873, it was finally forbidden to all Native Americans by the federal government; a ban which continued until the 1930s!

Today, in spite of this, Sweat Lodges are growing in popularity. Increasingly, non-native peoples are also discovering their deep healing power. It is important to realise, however, that leading a Sweat Lodge Ceremony is a serious undertaking to which one is traditionally called by a vision. It can be dangerous, and the leader of a Sweat is responsible for the physical and spiritual well-being of all the participants.

EXERCISE: SMUDGING

Smudging, or 'Sweeping the Smoke', is a simple but powerful method of purification, often used before other Native American Ceremonies. Look through the information in Chapter 4 and choose the herb or combination of herbs that you wish to use. Sage is a traditional choice because it is the strongest cleansing herb. Use your hands to roll the herb, imparting into it any prayers you feel appropriate. Place the rolled herb in a pot or shell. Burn the herb until it smoulders, giving off clouds of smoke.

'Smudging' with burning herbs and a feather

Use a Medicine Feather, or your hand, to circulate the smoke from the smouldering herb. Honour the seven directions – north, south, east, west, Father Sky, Mother Earth and Great Spirit at the centre of all. Bathe yourself, or someone you are working with, in the purifying smoke. Start from the bottom of the body and work up to the head. When you reach the top, flick the feather, or your hand, to remove any negative *energies* that the smoke may have removed from the person's 'aura'. Do this four times, circling the person in a clockwise direction. When you have finished, thank the *energies* and affirm *mitakuye oyasin* – 'we are all related'.

Objects and places can also be purified and made sacred in

this way. The interaction of the particular herb, the particular feather and your inner intention will give this ceremony its specific quality. You may use a special 'smudge stick' made of sage or cedar, in which case you will not require a pot to contain the loose herb or feather, but can simply 'Sweep the Smoke' by moving the stick.

WA'NA'NEE'CHE'S BALANCING TECHNIQUE

After you have prepared and purified yourself by smudging, this next exercise will bring balance and harmony to spirit, mind and body. It will help your energies reach a level where the body can naturally heal itself of any ailments. You cannot use this technique alone, but need to work with someone else. The one who feels they have the strongest *energy* should start by being the 'giver' and the other should be the 'receiver'. After the receiver has been *energized*, you may swap roles.

The giver should place their palms together and rub them vigorously to build up the *energies*. When the centre of the palms start to rise in temperature, place them on the head of the receiver, the left hand on the back of the skull and the right over the forehead – 'the third eye'. At the same time, call on the *energies* that are needed to bring healing. Concentrate on pushing *energy* down through the left hand to the base of the spine, and pulling it up again into the right hand. After some time, release the left hand and move the thumb and first two fingers of the right hand to the base of the nose. With this hand, pull out the negative *energies*. Flick them off your hand to remove them.

LAMENTING FOR A VISION

> Let us see, is this real,
> Let us see, is this real,
> This life I am living?
> You, Spirits, you dwell everywhere,
> Let us see, is this real,
> This life I am living?

PAWNEE SONG

Black Elk says 'the real world is behind this one, and everything we see here is something like a shadow from that world.' The 'real world' he is referring to is the unseen world of *spirit*, which can be perceived through mystical and visionary experiences.

In all cultures, and at all times in history, men and women have received visions; sometimes actively sought through spiritual practises like meditation, prayer, pilgrimage and so on; often unsolicited and even unwelcome. The people of Turtle Island consciously sought these experiences by drumming, dancing and singing; by ingesting psychedelic plants, fungi and toad secretions; by performing long sacred ceremonies; by putting themselves in great danger; by fasting and going on the Vision Quest.

The great Sioux visionary Black Elk in 1931 (*Joseph Epes Brown;*
from Animals of the Soul *by Joseph Epes Brown, reproduced*
courtesy Element Books, Shaftsbury, Dorset)

The visionary experiences of great mystics have shaped and
deepened our collective understanding of what it is to be alive.
These direct personal communications with *spirit* form the
bedrock of even the most worldly religious traditions. For the
people of Turtle Island, who have no written scriptures to turn
to as revelation by proxy, the ongoing direct communication

with the 'other world' was seen as essential and fundamental. Speaking in 1854, the Dwamish Chief Seattle said:

> Our religion is the traditions of our ancestors – the dreams of our old men, given to them in solemn hours of night by the Great Spirit; and the visions of our sachems (medicine people); and it is written in the hearts of the people.

DREAMS AND VISIONS

There are many types of 'vision' and many levels to the visionary world. The most common and universally experienced is dreaming. For us in the modern world, this process is usually just the release of stress and personal projections. Such dreams are often incoherent, vague and easily forgotten. Contrast these with how Black Elk speaks of his Great Vision:

> ...nothing I have ever seen with my eyes was so clear and bright as what my vision showed me; and no words that I have ever heard with my ears were like the words I heard. I did not have to remember these things; they have remembered themselves all these years. It was as I grew older that the meanings came clearer and clearer out of the pictures and the words; and even now I know that more was shown to me than I can tell.

A vision may occur whilst asleep or awake, and sometimes during illness. It will have clarity and meaning. It impresses itself upon consciousness and carries a sense of its importance. A vision is more fully sensual than an ordinary dream, and is usually in bright colours. It often contains one key detail which is a message to be contemplated and lived with. The people of Turtle Island did not view these visions as symbols of the personal, unconscious mind, but as communications from a shared reality that lies beyond our normal waking experience. They were not part of an 'alternative reality', but a wider experience of the One Reality.

In their dreams, the people of Turtle Island would see the place where the game was gathered, which would guide them in their hunting. They would visit distant relatives, or see a stranger approaching and be able to predict his time of arrival, sometimes days in advance. Because these people lived and thought as a community, such dreams became common property, to be discussed and interpreted by the whole tribe. It was not uncommon for more than one person to have the same dream. However, a dreamer would never relate the whole of his dream, for it was believed that in that way he could retain the dream's power and energy.

THE LANGUAGE OF SPIRIT

Native Americans experienced dreams and visions as communications from the spirits, or from Great Spirit. Sometimes these communications are in words; more often they are in symbols and images – the language of the world of *spirit*. Visions should not necessarily be taken literally. For example, images of death may actually prefigure spiritual rebirth or transformation. It may take time and the help of a Spiritual Advisor to translate the vocabulary of the visionary communication. Such experiences are often like seeds, from which the meaning 'grows' over time, in the same organic way that everything in life matures and develops.

Ultimately, the great Native American medicine teachers, like all great mystics, point us beyond symbols and visions, to the deep understanding that is latent in silence and stillness. This is experienced unconsciously by us all in the total rest of deep sleep – the stillness that lies behind both the seen world and the unseen world. The Sioux Medicine Man Lame Deer says the *wicasa wakan* wraps silence around him like a blanket. As Black Elk puts it: 'Is not silence the very voice of the Great Spirit?'

WA'NA'NEE'CHE'S TEACHINGS ON TYPES OF VISION

Wa'Na'Nee'Che' says that when one is receiving a vision, *energy* leaves the body and goes to a spiritual place where teachings are given. These could be teachings about the past – to recover wisdom that has been lost; or the present – to learn how to apply that wisdom today; or the future – to see into things to come. In a vision where a spirit helper is behind you, the vision relates to the past. In a vision where the helper appears in front of you, the vision relates to the future.

Visions of the future come in three types. Firstly, 'Walking Visions'. These are often experienced as 'deja vu' – the feeling of 'remembering' an event which is happening now. Here the vision is not recalled until it actually occurs, but the person has been unconsciously prepared for a future event which they recognize when they 'walk into it'.

Secondly, 'Warning Visions'. These are premonitions of a coming event – often unpleasant. These events can be encouraged to happen, or avoided. 'Destiny' is, in this sense, better understood as 'destination'. The premonition is a vision of the destination we will reach if there is no change of direction – just as a driver on a particular road may look at a map and see the city they will arrive at if they stay on the same road. Two-Leggeds have the freedom to change direction, and so alter their destination, or 'destiny'.

When such a vision refers to the one who has the vision, then how they respond to it is a personal matter. But when the vision refers to others, difficult moral dilemmas about interfering in the destiny of others are opened up. Wa'Na'Nee'Che' is clear that he feels we have no right to intrude on the lives of others, even to prevent a seeming disaster; that we do not know the unfolding of the greater picture that only the Creator can perceive. But this is a decision each recipient of a Warning Vision must answer for themselves.

The third type of 'future' vision teaches us about our personal gifts and how to use them, or something of our particular purpose in this life. Sometimes, as was the case with Black Elk, this can take a lifetime to understand. It is often necessary to work with someone who can interpret a vision, in order to glean its true meaning. Often the visionary wants to understand the vision now! They may invent an interpretation, instead of allowing it to arise naturally. As a general rule, Wa'Na'Nee'Che' recommends: 'the less you think and the more you feel, the more you will understand.'

PEYOTE VISIONS

The use of peyote to induce visions is a comparatively recent ceremony in North America. It was introduced just over a hundred years ago from the south, some say through the Apache, at a time when the indigenous peoples and their traditional ways were being destroyed by the White Man. Into this cultural chaos came the magical peyote, bringing new hope for a regeneration of the Old Ways. It gave birth to a pan-tribal movement called 'The Native American Church' or 'The Tipi Way' – a synthesis of southern peyote shamanism, indigenous northern traditions and European Christianity.

This church is served by 'Road Men', who are like travelling priests, moving from place to place conducting Peyote

Ceremonies. The use of peyote is seen by many as a way to combat the alcoholism, apathy, poverty and loss of cultural identity that has plagued modern Native American peoples. Today this church is growing in strength, and the ceremonial use of peyote has recently been made legal across the United States.

Peyote is a powerful psychoactive cactus used by shamans in the south to communicate with *Mescalito* – a Spirit Ally. It is said to open up a doorway into the unseen world. A Washoe follower of the 'Tipi Way' says:

> The whole world is in there. When I am looking at this fine little peyote here my mind is praying. I can't think of nothing bad. All is good. It shows you everything there is to see ... all the people in the world ... all the different animals ... all the places ... It shows you all that's in the sky ... everything under this earth here ... It makes your eyes like x-rays so you can see what's inside things. You can see inside a person and see if he is in good health or he got some sickness in there. It makes your mind like a telegram. You can send your thoughts far away to some other person and that person can send messages to you ... It is the music the Creator put on earth to make the minds of humans good and clear.

The Water Bird, or Peyote Bird, is the totem of the Peyote Ceremony. This Medicine Bird is said to see its reflection in the water below it. Likewise, peyote is said to give the gift of self-reflection. It gives the user the ability to see into himself; to perceive his inner light; to deal with his inner 'darkness' and fear in the safe, supportive, ceremonial context of prayer and singing.

Many Medicine People, such as Wa'Na'Nee'Che', do not support the use of peyote; not just because it is not a traditional practice, but because they feel the peyote vision is not a true vision. It is, they believe, heavily contaminated with projections from the personal psyche. The peyote is not necessary to gain visions, they argue, so why use it? The peyote user would reply that it is a sacred plant, given by Great Spirit. If used with reverence it gives powerful visions that are not random or strange, but recognizably transcendental. For someone observing this debate about the ceremonial use of peyote from the outside, it is important to separate it completely from the arguments about the pleasures and dangers of 'recreational drug use'. Psychoactive plants have always formed an important part of shamanic culture all over the world.

Perhaps the modern world has such a tragic relationship with these plants, and the substances we have synthesized from them, because we have no understanding of their spiritual dimension. We do not treat them as sacred. We do not prepare ourselves to partake in them. We treat them as an inconsequential way to get a quick and easy 'high'. Like tobacco – a sacred herb used for healing by indigenous people – these substances have become abused by our lack of respect and have turned from allies into enemies. Once again, our modern 'problem' is the result of stripping away the sacred aspect of a benevolent part of Creation, and we are the losers. We no longer have visionaries – we have junkies!

For followers of the Tipi Way, the peyote is not a means to personal gratification and mindless intoxication. As a peyote user says:

In this Tipi Way Church the people get together for the good of everybody. Each person don't work just for himself. He can't use the Medicine for that. He got to think of his family, all them other ones there in the Tipi ... and he got to think good of all the other people in the world, even the ones who is against him.

THE VISION QUEST

In the old days, tribes all over Turtle Island believed that visionary experience was essential to living a full life. For some, such as the tribes west of the Rocky Mountains, visions and guardian spirits usually came without having to be asked. For most, however, the vision was actively sought with some form of Vision Quest. Amongst some of the south-western people, and those nearer the Arctic, this special spiritual retreat was undertaken only by those seeking the powers of a Medicine Person, or 'Singer', as they are called by the Navajo and Apache.

Amongst other tribes, a Vision Quest was undertaken by anyone seeking a Guardian Spirit, or seeking to find answers to personal or tribal predicaments. The great Sioux leader Crazy Horse, for example, was renowned for disappearing in search of visionary guidance, in order to comprehend how best to deal with the danger of the White Invaders. Often a Vision Quest was undertaken as a compulsory part of the initiation from boyhood into manhood; less often at the maturity of a young woman. The practice was most developed amongst the Plains Peoples. The Lakota Sioux called it 'Lamenting for a Vision' or 'Crying for a Dream'.

Throughout history, seekers of visions have retreated from their day-to-day life into the wilderness, to those places most alive with the power of Nature. Moses went to the summit of Mount Sinai and received the ten commandments. Jesus went into the desert for forty days and forty nights to face the temptations of the Devil. For the followers of some religions, it is enough that someone else has done this for them. For the people of the Plains it was necessary for each individual to seek this experience for himself. Black Elk says that in the old days, men and women 'lamented' all the time. No one, it was

PREPARING FOR A VISION QUEST

A Vision Quest is a serious business, not to be taken lightly. When the time is right, a quester will feel called by the spirits to 'go on the hill'. They will seek out the guidance of a *Wicasa Wakan* – someone with intimate knowledge of the unseen world. If things are not done correctly, the quest could potentially be very dangerous for both body and spirit.

If the aspirant is seen to be ready, he will start a period of preparation that traditionally can last weeks or even a year. He will purify himself with fasting, prayer and the ceremonial use of the Sweat Lodge. When the time comes, his Spiritual Advisor will lead him to a specially chosen, isolated place on a mountain or a hilltop. The wilderness is dangerous and remote. It is a place where Nature speaks, unfettered by human interference.

GOING ON THE HILL

Traditionally, the quester, or lamenter, will stay in this place for four days and four nights – although sometimes a single night is a shorter form of the same experience. The exact procedures vary and some are secret, but generally the aspirant must commit to remain alone without food or water, exposed to the elements, until he receives his vision. He has nothing but a blanket against the cold, and perhaps a sacred pipe or the contents of his medicine bundle to aid him in his prayers. He faces fear, loneliness and doubt. This is a time of trial; an initiation after which he will never be the same again.

Sometimes a quester is given a secret 'energy tea' by the

Medicine Person who acts as their guide. This slows down his body functions and helps him retain water. The quester may have to stay within a specially prescribed circle, probably made of tobacco ties prepared before 'going on the hill', each one containing a prayer for the Quest. He may on no account leave this circle. During these days and nights, he must focus continually on his desire for a vision. Ideally he should not sleep, but if he does, any dreams must be remembered. He must be attentive to every small event, so that he can recall it later, when his Spiritual Advisor will decode it with him.

The Medicine Person is responsible for the safety of the lamenter who he has agreed to guide. He remains hidden somewhere near by and guards a fire, offering prayers, performing rituals to aid the Quest and possibly fasting himself. He makes sure that the four elements – earth, air, fire and water – are all ceremonially present. He will remain there until the lamenter receives a vision. Some Vision Quest Guides, like the contemporary Medicine Man Frank Fool's Crow, are also able to see the vision as it is received by the person under their care.

The aspirant prays and sings sacred songs. In some traditions he performs hard manual labour, like lifting heavy stones, to weaken his body and open him up to the visionary world. In the old days, he may have cut pieces of his flesh, or even cut off a finger as a sacrifice. Sometimes he would have been given a number of squares of skin, cut by a grandmother from her own arm, as an offering to the spirits so they might assist the lamenter in his Quest, and so that her bravery would inspire him to face his fears.

THE NIGHT OF FEAR

In some Native American Traditions, the seeker will first have undergone 'The Night of Fear' as a preparation for the Vision Quest. This death/rebirth ritual is designed to bring out all the unconscious fears of the participant, so that he may face and overcome them. It involves going to a remote spot and digging one's own grave!

The lamenter will lie in this 'grave' throughout the night, covered completely by a blanket. The sounds of the night, and the inability to see, naturally stimulate him into imagining all kinds of terrors lurking around him. The lamenter is confront- ed very directly with his own mortality – the root of all fear. If he can find his inner courage, he may come to a personal, intu- itive knowledge of his spiritual immortality.

RECEIVING A VISION

Not every lamenter receives a vision or a visit from a Spirit Ally – but many do. Visions often come as an animal, or in some other natural form. The lamenter may hear whispering voices in the moaning wind; or be visited by a wild deer; or a particu- lar flower may keep catching his eye as if it were calling to him; or an eagle may fly down into his circle; or he may dream of the mythical Thunderbird or the Sacred Buffalo. The spirit of this animal or plant is offering itself to be his helper.

According to a legend of the Pawnee, a great council of all the animals, called *Nahurac*, constantly meets in a cave under a round mountain called *Pahok*. These animals watch over the whole world, and if they see a man or woman calling for assis- tance with true humility, the council will choose one of their number – a Winged One or a Four-Legged, or a Crawling Person – to appear to the human supplicant and guide him in his life, or share with him its particular Medicine Power.

The lamenter becomes identified with the animal that has come to him. He may pledge never to take the life of one of its kind. He will carry something to remind him of this animal at all times; perhaps a feather, a skin, or a shield painting. By studying the nature of this animal, the lamenter will discover his own gifts and talents – his own place in the Circle of Life. Someone with a spiritual connection with the attractive and beguiling deer, for example, will share its 'Love Medicine'. He may have the power to attract the opposite sex or to heal broken hearts. Someone else may have the power to heal with a certain herb. Another may have the eagle's ability to see things clearly.

There are stories of young men who have become so frightened or impatient on their quest, that they have taken their first encounter with an animal to be the final fruit of their endeavours, and so returned to the tribe. There are other tales of lamenters who have held out for a stronger vision, and been blessed at last by a powerful Spirit Ally who has given them a new sacred name, with associated Medicine Powers; perhaps to heal the sick, or lead the people, or be protected in war. They may also have received a sacred Medicine Song, to be sung at times of need or danger, when they can call up their guardian spirit and remind themselves of the inner strength they found in their Vision Quest.

Other lamenters relate how they persevered, even when visited by a wild animal that allowed them to pet it or even talked to them! The reward for this endurance has sometimes been a vision of Great Spirit, in a human form or simply as light. On the other hand, there are myths and stories of lamenters who ignored visits from a seemingly insignificant visitor such as an ant – waiting for a buffalo, an eagle or some other more 'important' spirit – only to discover that this ant was indeed Great

LIVING A VISION

The Vision Quest often ends as it began, in the purification ceremony of the Sweat Lodge. The lamenter shares his experiences with his Spiritual Advisor, who helps him intuitively understand their meaning. In many traditions he must now publicly externalize his vision, perhaps through song or dance or a shield painting. As Black Elk says:

A man who has a vision is not able to use the power of it until after he has performed the vision on the earth for the people to see.

When important and powerful visions were experienced, like those seen by Black Elk, the whole tribe would come together to act out the vision, each taking various parts, like participants in a great psychodrama. For a young person, receiving a vision was an initiation – the beginning of the rest of his life. He would probably have received a new name, and he now had a Spirit Ally that he could call upon in times of need. He had more knowledge of his gifts, and of his place in the circle of the tribe and the wider Circle of Life. His challenge now was to let the seed of his vision grow within him, to eventually yield the fruit of spiritual wisdom. For some, like Black Elk, who was very young when he received his great vision, this can be a heavy responsibility; it is not always easy to live up to the truths it has been our gift to perceive.

THE VISION QUEST TODAY

Today, many native and non-native people undertake a Vision Quest. It is important however, to have a skilled and responsible spiritual guide. It is also important to remember that the average modern person does not have the physical stamina that characterized Native Americans in the past, who lived most of their lives outside, performing strenuous physical tasks; drinking clean water, breathing clean air, eating healthy food. Because of these differences, contemporary guides often do not demand such rigorous fasting. A modern person may be given water, for example, simply to wash through all the toxins that are being released into the bloodstream as their body purifies.

EXERCISE: A VISION JOURNEY

For those who do not have the opportunity to go on a Vision Quest under the guidance of an experienced Medicine Person, a 'Vision Journey' is a simple and safe elementary introduction to exploring the visionary experience. Many contemporary Native American teachers, such as Wa'Na'Nee'Che', work with their students using these types of inner imagination techniques. Ideally you should do this exercise with a friend, one of you being the 'guide', who will help the other into the vision world. Different people 'visualize' in different ways. For some it is vague, for others very clear. This doesn't matter. Pay attention to the feelings and images as they appear to you. Don't force things, and don't worry if at first you find the exercise strange or difficult. Begin by lying down in a comfortable position, closing your eyes and allowing yourself to relax.

If possible, hit a drum synchronized to the rhythm of your heart beat. At first the drumbeat should be strong and loud, falling slowly down to a gentle, soothing tap. Whilst still quietly drumming, read the following text. While you do this, try and 'tune in' intuitively to the person you are guiding, so you can feel when to read slowly and when to speed up; how long to pause; when to give them time to explore their imagination; when to continue leading them on:

Use the power of your imagination to visualize a door in front of you. Pass through this door and find yourself in a beautiful wild forest, surrounded by fine tall trees, lush vegetation and bright flowers. Shafts of warm sunlight are breaking through the leaves above you, showering the woodland with sunbeams. Before you is a path leading into the depths of the forest. The breeze is gently rustling the leaves and you feel as if you can hear the Standing People calling you to follow the path.

Go down the path until you arrive at a clearing. (PAUSE).

Walk around the clearing in a circle until you find 'your place'. When you find the spot that is calling you, sit here and humbly offer up prayers to Great Spirit for help and guidance. (PAUSE).

As you wait, an animal will appear from amongst the trees. Listen carefully and it may speak to you. You may wish to ask it a question. (PAUSE).

As you watch, the animal form changes into the white light of Great Spirit, which reaches out to you, bathing you in love and peace. (PAUSE).

Gradually the light fades. Look down, and at your feet you will see you have been left a gift. It may be a herb, or a medicine tool, or a crystal. (PAUSE).

Pick up the gift and, with gratitude in your heart, prepare for your journey back.

When you feel the time is right, start to increase the strength and volume of the drumbeat. Tell the person you have been guiding to become more aware of the seen world – then finally to open their eyes and stretch their body.

AFTER THE JOURNEY

Immediately, write down all that you have experienced on your Journey, so that nothing is forgotten. You may want to share this with a Spiritual Advisor, if you have one. It is also useful to be able to refer back to this experience at some future date. Take some time to contemplate your personal associations with the animal that appeared to you. You may want to read some books and find out more about this animal. Contemplate your gift. What is its *energy*? What spiritual qualities does it embody for you? Does it mean anything to you in your life at the moment? Dwell on this experience over the next few days, and allow its meaning to grow inside you.

COMPLETING THE CIRCLE

And when the last Red Man shall have perished,
and the memory of my tribe
shall have become a myth among the White Men,
these shores will swim
with the invisible dead of my tribe,
and when your children's children
think themselves alone
in the field, the store, the shop,
upon the highway,
or in the silence of the pathless wood,
they will not be alone.
At nights when the streets of your cities
and villages are silent
and you think them deserted,
they will throng with the returning hosts
that once filled and still love this beautiful land.
The White Man will never be alone.
Let him be just and deal kindly with my people,
for the dead are not powerless.
Dead did I say?
There is no death, only a change of worlds

CHIEF SEATTLE, 1854

The traditions, culture and natural wisdom of the Red Man have indeed been taken to the edge of extinction.

But despite genocide and persecution, they have survived – and more than survived – they are today coming alive once more to meet the needs of new generations. For Native Americans, this poses new challenges. For some, the important thing is to preserve their traditional ways, before they are forgotten for ever. Like other subjugated nations, the indigenous people of Turtle Island need to proudly remember the history of their great culture, in order to have a sense of who they are and where they have come from. If these traditions are allowed to become lost, we will all be the poorer for it.

For other modern Native Americans, among them Wa'Na'Nee'Che', it is not the maintenance of traditions that is of primary importance, but the eternal truths they represent. For him, and others like him, it is the living spirit of the 'Old Ways' that must be rediscovered and re-expressed in a manner that suits the present realities of life. Native American Spirituality is not a relic to be preserved in a cultural museum for the curiosity of future generations. To stay alive it must be vibrant and able to grow organically to meet the new challenges of the modern world.

Native American ways are changing – but they have always done so. The great cultures of the Plains Peoples, for example, largely came about through tribes from the east being forced further west by the advancing White Invaders. It is hard to say what is culturally 'pure' and what is the product of the interpenetration of indigenous and European cultures. For Wa'Na'Nee'Che', traditional Native American ways are themselves only the remnants of the 'Old Ways' that had already been lost by the time the White Man came.

Practices like the Sweat Lodge were persecuted for so many years that it is understandably difficult for some Native

Americans to see them now being embraced by the White Man – like the latest fashion – and to watch modern indigenous teachers popularizing their sacred traditions amongst their one-time enemies. But many tribes had predicted that one day the White Man would turn in need to the indigenous peoples. That need is here and that day is coming. If we have patience and humility, perhaps the great wounds of the past can be healed with the *medicine* of understanding and forgiveness. Wa'Na'Nee'Che' says, 'The only thing that keeps us apart is communication', which is a delightfully ambiguous statement!

THE MYTH OF THE RED MAN .

As Chief Seattle predicted, the Red Man has become like a myth to the White Man. First he was portrayed as the cruel savage of the 'Cowboys and Indians' stories; an evolutionary leftover of 'primitive man', from whom sophisticated modern man has developed. More recently he has become the 'noble savage', vividly portrayed in the film *Dances with Wolves*: honest and brave, connected to Nature, caring for Mother Earth, living on vast, open plains that teem with wild animals.

It is easy to dismiss this latest myth as sentimental, and just as unrealistic as the former. But in some ways, the modern world needs this idealistic vision right now. We need a new myth to live by. As we choke on the smoke of our polluted cities – living lives cut off from each other, and from nature, and from the Great Mystery of Life – we need to remember that things haven't always been this way; not so that we can simply idealize the past, but so that we can reappraise the present and change our collective destiny.

If the dead of Turtle Island are indeed walking the streets of our cities, as Chief Seattle predicted, then they will know the price we are paying for ignoring their perennial wisdom. They will have seen the alienation and confusion that so many people feel today. We have created what the Hopi call *Koyaanisquatsi* – 'life-out-of-balance'. With modern exploration and technology we have united the world: we can visit the farthest shore in hours; we can communicate across continents at the press of a button. But with our weapons, industrial pollution and relentless exploitation of Nature, we are in danger of ripping the very Web of Life.

Our Earth is dying because we no longer believe She is alive. To the modern mind, the very idea seems absurd. But we have lost our connection with *spirit* and everything has become absurd! By seeing so much of Creation as 'inanimate', we have left ourselves a dead world to live in. Perhaps this is why we have been able to destroy so much of it – without seeming to notice. For the Native American, the Creator is embodied within His Creation; when the White Man recklessly wastes so many natural resources, he is wasting God.

We see ourselves as subduing Nature for our own ends, not working with Her or for Her. We have replaced a mother/child relationship with one of master/slave. We have replaced the spiritual purification of the Ceremonial Sweat Lodge with the convenience of the Health Suite Sauna. We don't use sacred tobacco and peyote to touch the Great Mystery, we 'escape' with 'drugs', and the result is cancer and addiction. We put those who have visions on Valium, or in sanatoriums.

We have divorced ourselves from *spirit*. Perhaps this is why we feel an emptiness inside us. Although we have gained all our 'knowledge' from a meticulous study of Nature, we have failed to learn Her 'wisdom'. We know much about the world, but little about ourselves. We may know *how* things are, but we have forgotten *why* things are. For the ancient peoples, the roots of human life are nourished by the unseen world. By ignoring the spiritual foundation of things, everything we build is out of balance, unstable, and will eventually crumble and fall about us.

The modern world has two influential philosophies: mainstream Christianity, which divorces the *spirit* world from the physical world, and scientific materialism, which denies the existence of *spirit* all together. But step back, if you can, from the cultural prejudices of our own brief age, and remember that at any other time in history it would be our modern beliefs and attitudes that would be thought strange and foolish. Chief Seattle says:

> This we know: The earth does not belong to man, man belongs to the earth. All things are connected like the blood which unites us all. Man did not weave the Web of Life, he is merely a strand in it. Whatever he does to the Web, he does to himself.

RETURNING TO THE GOOD RED ROAD

How are we to find once again the Good Red Road? Native Americans who felt out of balance would attempt to realign themselves with the pre-existing harmony of their tribe. We cannot do this, for it is our society itself which is out of balance. In a consumerist culture which worships commerce, those who do find their spiritual gifts are often not valued and can find no place. How then can we live in the 'Old Ways'?

How shall we learn to walk with reverence on the earth, when it is covered in concrete? How can we be taught by the wilderness, when we live in vast sprawling cities? Even in the countryside, the only animals we can commune with are domesticated. It is hard to see a great teaching *spirit* within the sheep or cows we have reared as if they were products in a factory.

The lives the Native Americans lived were contained by the spirit world. Their dwellings were more than functional or beautiful; they spoke, symbolically, of a deeper reality. The designs on their clothing, the construction of their artefacts, their ways of relating – all reminded them of the unseen world. When the People of Turtle Island built a Sweat Lodge, they saw beyond the elements used in its construction, to the metaphysical *energies* these elements embodied. It is difficult to imagine finding this level of spiritual awareness in any modern activity.

Could we see through to the 'mythic' reality when driving a car? Could we see this tin box as a 'living being' with a *spirit* and powerful *medicine*? It is surely part of life and must therefore be part of the Great Mystery. It could remind us that our bodies are like vehicles within which we move, but which we will eventually leave for scrap. As we pour in the petrol, we could remember that we are using power taken from within Mother Earth to fire up the engine. As we drive we could remember that we are free to change our 'destiny', in the same way that we can change the 'destination' we are motoring towards.

The problem is that we know something is wrong; that in some major way all of this is out of balance. If we allowed ourselves to fully enter into a spiritual awareness we would be forced to acknowledge all the fundamental disharmony that surrounds us, and might well not drive our car at all. If we communed with the spirits of the livestock on our farms, we would have to face the shame of what we have made them. If their spirits could speak to us, would they come to guide us, or chide us?

It is ironic that we who have lived by the straight line; we who have seen time as inexorably 'progressing' along a straight evolutionary path from the lesser to the better; we who have divided up the earth saying 'beyond this line is mine and not yours'; we who have carved monumental, straight motorways across the countryside so we can travel directly 'from a to b'; we are the ones who have discovered, by our restless exploration, that the earth is round! We have journeyed into the stars and looked back upon our planet as a beautiful blue, spherical Whole. We have concluded, by the logic of our *medicine* powers of science and technology, that space itself is curved! Perhaps the solution to the modern dilemmas we have created by our logical, linear thought, is to think in circles, as the primal peoples do.

A circle represents the Whole. We live on one earth and the forest felled by one country damages the environment of another. The air polluted here is the same air breathed by all. Nature is no longer allowing us to live in the illusion of our separateness. The disaster of the environmental crisis is forcing us to re-examine our image of ourselves as self-serving individuals, and acknowledge our essential interdependence. If we are to become one human family, it will be by acknowledging that we all share one Mother Earth.

A circle embraces – a line divides. Native American traditions allocate the colours red, black, yellow and white to the four quarters of the Circle of Life. These colours represent the different races of humanity. By uniting them into one human tribe, maybe we can overcome the divisions that have caused so much suffering – not unified in one market place or in one colourless monoculture, but as the different spokes of one wheel: each of equal value, just as every point on the circumference of a circle is of equal distance from the centre.

The circle is a symbol of balance. Wisdom is 'knowledge in balance'. Perhaps it is not because of our new technological knowledge that we have so many problems, but because we do not use this knowledge in a balanced relationship with the Whole of Life. If you observe your own personality, and the people around you, you will often see that a person's greatest quality when they are 'in balance' will be their greatest problem when they are 'out of balance'. A great leader, for instance, may have a tendency to become arrogant or dominant. An eloquent speaker may become manipulative. A sensitive carer may become a doormat. Our modern culture has many strengths, but as these are out of balance with the Whole they have become vast problems.

Most importantly, a circle has a centre. A wheel revolves around an axle. If our modern culture can centre itself in an awareness of the Great Sacred Mystery of Life, perhaps the technological power that has created so many problems can be used in balance. Perhaps it may turn out to be the very *medicine* that will co-create, with Great Spirit, the new Golden Age of so many indigenous prophecies.

The people of Turtle Island say that time is a circle. Perhaps we do not have to 'go back' to find lost wisdom, or rush forward in search of a better future. Perhaps if we simply find the spiritual centre of balance and harmony in the present moment, we will discover that the 'Old Ways' are not only hidden in our distant past – they are also calling in our immediate future.

But how can we spiritually 'centre' our culture? Only by centring ourselves. The Native Americans teach that when an individual is out of balance, all they touch becomes out of balance. Likewise when they are in harmony, all they touch becomes harmonized. The unseen world is the world of our intentions and motivations. Every one of our thoughts and actions arises from the unseen world and sends ripples through the seen world, like a stone thrown into a pool of water. If we can centre ourselves in *spirit*, then the ripples we leave behind us will become expanding circles of healing.

THE HOOP WILL COME TOGETHER

As a young man, Black Elk was present at the massacre of Wounded Knee. As he surveyed the torn and broken bodies of his people, he knew that the Sacred Hoop was broken – the Sacred Tree was dead. Many years later, as an old man, he asked his biographer, John G. Neihardt, to take him up to Harvey Peak. In his youth he had been brought here by the spirits in a great vision that had shaped his life; a vision he felt he had failed to live up to, with a shame that filled his soul. When they reached the summit he turned to his son Ben, and said quietly:

> Something should happen today. If I only have a little power left, the Thunder Beings of the West should hear me when I send a voice, and there should be a little rain.

The day was clear and cloudless. It was the dry season. Black Elk honoured the four directions and sent forth a thin, pathetic voice which flew upward to Great Spirit: 'Hey-a-a-hey! Hey-a-a-hey!'. Small clouds began mysteriously to form above his head. There was a rumble of thunder without lightning, and the old man stood gently weeping as drops of rain began to fall. Neihardt stood astonished as the rain, mingling now with the old man's tears, fell onto the parched land: a land that Black Elk and his people had loved so much, and which had been taken from them so brutally.

It only takes a little rain for the Sacred Tree to sprout new green shoots, for wisdom may be forgotten, but never lost.

Black Elk felt he had failed his vision, but perhaps he unknowingly bequeathed it to us today – as a source of inspiration, so we may never forget Great Spirit, and the wisdom and the suffering of the People of Turtle Island.

Wallace Black Elk is a contemporary Lakota *wicasa wakan*, and a pipe-bearing descendant of the great Black Elk. I will complete the circle of this book by ending with his words:

> Purification will come
> and grandma will cradle us
> in her arms
> and wipe away our tears
> and grandpa will walk among us.
> It will be this generation
> you people
> will make it reality
> and the hoop
> will come together again.
>
> – MITAKUYE OYASIN –

FURTHER READING

As I have not been able to go deeply into all aspects of Native American wisdom, I have listed a selection of books that more thoroughly explore particular areas of interest.

Neihardt, John. *Black Elk Speaks*, University of Nebraska Press. A wonderfully inspiring account of the life of the great Sioux visionary.

Brown, Dee. *Bury My Heart At Wounded Knee*, Vintage. An excellent history of the Indian Wars.

Brown, Joseph Epes. *The Spiritual Legacy Of The American Indian*, Crossroad. A scholarly exploration of Native American Spirituality.

Storm Hyemeyohsts. *Seven Arrows*, Ballantine Books. An inspiring book, with many beautiful pictures.

Bruchac, Joseph. *The Native American Sweat Lodge*, Crossing P. A detailed look at the Sweat Lodge.

Edmonds, Margot, Clark, Ella E and Braun, Molly. *Voices Of The Winds*, Facts on File. Native American myths and legends.

Peat, F. David. *Blackfoot Physics*, Fourth Estate. A fascinating look at Native American wisdom through the eyes of a modern physicist.

comp. Turner, Frederick W. *The Portable North American Reader*, Penguin. A good anthology of writings by and about Native Americans.

comp. Nicholson, Shirley. *Shamanism*, Quest Books. An excellent collection of articles on the Shamanic beliefs and practices of the Primal Peoples.

L. d'Azevedo, Warren L. (ed.) *Straight With The Medicine*, Heyday Books. First-hand accounts of Peyote experiences.